Strategic Missile Forces of the Russian Federation

Organisation and Missile Complexes

Hugh Harkins

Copyright © 2021 Hugh Harkins FRAS, MIstP, MRAeS

All rights reserved.

ISBN: 1-903630-94-0
ISBN-13: 978-1-903630-94-5

Strategic Missile Forces of the Russian Federation

Organisation and Missile Complexes

© 2021 Hugh Harkins FRAS, MIstP, MRAeS

Centurion Publishing

United Kingdom

ISBN 10: 1-903630-94-0
ISBN 13: 978-1-903630-94-5

This volume first published in 2021

The Author is identified as the copyright holder of this work under sections 77 and 78 of the Copyright Designs and Patents Act 1988

Cover design © Centurion Publishing & KDP

Page layout, concept and design © Centurion Publishing

All rights reserved. No part of this publication may be reproduced, stored in a retrieval system, transmitted in any form, or by any means, electronic, mechanical or photocopied, recorded or otherwise, without the written permission of the publisher

This volume has adopted a quasi-Harvard Manual of Style for referencing. It has, however, not always been possible to adopt a standard referencing format

CONTENTS

	Introduction	vii
1	Overview of the Strategic Missile Force(s) From Conception to the Twenty First Century	1
2	New START and the Russian Nuclear Posture	13
3	Missile Armies and Missile Divisions of the Strategic Missile Forces	17
4	Strategic Missile Forces Intercontinental Ballistic Missile Complexes	47
5	Missile Attack Warning System of the Missile Defence Forces	109
6	Strategic Missile Forces Development and Modernisation Under Defence Planning Covering 2012-2022	117
7	Glossary	131
8	Bibliography	133

INTRODUCTION

In the second and third decades of the twenty first century the Russian Federation Strategic Missile Forces, the largest arm of the Russian Strategic Nuclear Forces, underwent force modernisation to ensure deterrent capability to counter proliferation of North Atlantic Treaty Organisation missile defence systems. Capability enhancements and deterrence potential would be ensured through the introduction/development of advanced intercontinental ballistic missile complexes – Yars and Sarmat – armed with a new generation of maneuverable warheads, the Avangard hypersonic glide vehicle and, longer term, the projected Kedr light intercontinental ballistic missile, revealed in 2020.

The volume draws upon information from official sources to provide a picture of the Strategic Missile Forces and constituent missile systems as understood in early 2021 when it operated RT-2PM Topol, RT-2PM2/1 Topol-M, RS-24 Yars series, R-36M2, UR-100N UTTKh and Avangard complexes, with the RS-28 Sarmat then scheduled to be placed on alert the following year. In regard to Avangard and Sarmat, information is naturally scarce as these programs were, in 2021, shrouded in the highest levels of classification. However, significant data had been released to provide an informed outline of the systems, which, along with Yars, were intended to constitute the backbone of the Strategic Missile Forces through the third decade of the twenty first century.

The volume adopts a factual rather than a geopolitical approach and avoids unsubstantiated data. The number of strategic strike systems, ICBM complexes etc., in service and deployed, are taken directly from the data submitted by both parties to the New Strategic Arms Reduction Treaty. All technical data concerning missile complexes and associated systems, missile formations and associated organisations, operational data, such as the Russian Federations nuclear doctrine (thresholds for the use of nuclear weapons), along with graphic material, has been furnished by the respective design bureau, manufacturers, experimental/research agencies, the Ministry of Defence of the Russian Federation and the Ministry of Foreign Affairs of the Russian Federation.

1

OVERVIEW OF THE STRATEGIC MISSILE FORCE(S) FROM CONCEPTION TO THE TWENTY FIRST CENTURY

In 2021, the Russian Federation SMF (Strategic Missile Forces) constituted the largest of the three arms of that nation's deterrent Strategic Nuclear Forces triad of land based ICBM (Intercontinental Ballistic Missile) – silo and mobile groupings – SLBM (Submarine Launched Ballistic Missile) – carried on and launched from Russian Northern and Pacific Fleet nuclear armed nuclear powered underwater cruisers (ballistic missile submarines) – and air launched cruise missiles – carried on and launched from Tupolev Tu-160/M and Tu-95MS strategic missile carriers of Long Range Aviation. Over the decade or so into 2021, the SMF underwent significant modernisation through re-equipment with modern systems designed to ensure viability of the nuclear deterrent in the face of the proliferation of US (United States) missile defence systems. These systems had been deployed near Russia's western, southern and eastern borders and in the continental US non-contiguous state of Alaska, covering over the Arctic direction of ICBM flight.

The long-range ballistic missile force had been created by the USSR (Union of Soviet Socialist Republics/Soviet Union) to facilitate the delivery of special (atomic/nuclear) payloads against strategic and, ultimately, intercontinental range targets. This was achieved to offset NATO (North Atlantic Treaty Organisation), predominantly US, capability to deliver nuclear strikes at intercontinental range by its intercontinental and intermediate range bomber aircraft forces, which were significantly in advance of that of the Soviet Union in terms of numbers and strike potential. Ballistic missiles were considered by the Soviet Union as a more efficient means of ensuring destruction of an enemy in a retaliatory strike as they were difficult and, at the time of their introduction, impossible to defend against. This reinforced the nuclear strike option as a deterrent force by signaling to NATO that a nuclear first strike against the Soviet Union would be met with sufficient retaliatory strike potential to ensure destruction of major NATO strategic and population centres.

The creation of the Soviet SMF had been authorised under a USSR Council of Ministers Decree, *No.1384-615*, dated 17 December 1959. The 17th of December is officially recognised as the date of the creation of the SMF under the authority of a Russian Federation Presidential Decree, *No.1239*, dated 10 December 1995 and reinforced by Presidential Decree *No.549* of 31 May 2006 (MODRF SMF, 2017).

Launch of a 15ZH58 missile of an RT-2PM Topol fourth generation ICBM complex of the Russian Federation Strategic Missile Forces. MODRF

Creation of the SMF was proceeded by a decade and a half of intense Soviet activity in the fields of ballistic missile atomic bomb/warhead design/development. This was accomplished in the context of the USSR race to remove the threat of nuclear attack on her homeland with no prospect of responding in kind that had been introduced in the closing months of World War II with the July 1945 detonation of the world's first atomic bomb/device – the Manhattan Project Trinity test. The destruction caused by the relatively low yield (~15/21 kiloton (US Department of Energy)) atomic bombs dropped on Hiroshima and Nagasaki, Japan, in August 1945, left a mark on the Soviet Union, which endeavored to become a nuclear power in as short a time period as was possible to remove the advantage the US possessed in the new post-war world order.

In the early Cold War period – the decades immediately following the end of World War II – the US and USSR were vying for ballistic missile supremacy, with the added prize of access to space. An atmosphere of mutual mistrust would lead to several decades in which the respective power blocks (Soviet dominated Warsaw Pact and United States dominated NATO) existed under the spectre of nuclear Armageddon such as human kind had never before witnessed (Harkins, 2017).

The OKB-1 single-stage R-1 was the first operational Soviet ballistic missile. With a range of 270 km the R-1 fell into the category of what would come to be known as short-range ballistic missiles. The conventional warhead mass was 1075 kg. Energia

While this volume is not intended to serve as a history of Soviet rocket/ballistic missile development, an overview of such development milestones that would make creation of the SMF practical would be pertinent. It is an indisputable historical fact that the post war rocket programs in the Soviet Union and the United States that would lead to the dawn of the ICBM and space payload launch vehicles were born of the ashes of World War II Germany and, in particular, the A-4 (V-2) rocket, which was tested and further adapted by the Soviets and Americans in the immediate post war years. In the USSR, this would lead to a 14 April 1948 Soviet government decree authorising development of what would become the R-1, the first Soviet ballistic missile derived from the A-4 (FAU-2) (MODRF, Harkins, 2017 & Energia, 2016).

Development of the R-1 had been enabled by the formation of several test facilities and manufacturing centers under a decree of the Soviet government dated 13 May 1946. This was part of the overall effort to develop a long range ballistic missile under the direction of chief designer S.P. Korolev. A decree of the Soviet minister of armaments, D.F. Ustinov, issued on 26 August 1946, authorised the formation of an organisational structure under NII-88. This effectively put in place Department 3 of the Special Design Bureau, OKB-1, (now the S.P. Korolev Rocket and Space Corporation, Energia) under the leadership of Korolev. Korolev would go on become the architect of not only the Soviet Union's embryonic long range ballistic missile programs, but also that nations space launch vehicle programs that signaled the dawn of the space age (Harkins, 2017 & Energia, 2016).

The first Soviet launch of an A-4 (a missile assembled from various parts of captured German rockets) occurred on 18 October 1947. Soviet flight testing of the A-4 was concluded in late 1947 and the first R-1 launch was conducted on 17 September the following year. This launch was considered a failure. Although it almost achieved the specified design range, a malfunction of the off-nominal function of the control system sent the missile off course. The first completely successful launch and flight of an R-1 was conducted on 10 October 1948 and the first phase of R-1 flight testing was completed later that year, paving the way for the missile system to enter operational service in 1950. The R-1, with a maximum firing range of 270 km, would later fall into the group of missiles termed SRBM (Short-Range Ballistic Missile), which covered vehicles with a firing range up to 1109 km (599 nm). In a prelude to space flight testing, an R-1 derivative, the R-1A, was utilised from 21 April 1949, to launch a series of six upper atmospheric missions (altitudes of around 100 km) to release instrumented containers for atmospheric tests during the parachute descent (Harkins, 2017 & Energia, 2016).

The R-2E (Experimental) was launched on 21 September 1949, to test systems for the projected R-2 ballistic missile complex, which had a detachable nose cone for the warhead housing section – this missile complex entered service in 1951. Soviet missile developments of the late 1940's and early 1950's would lead to a multitude of designs, including the R-5, the first of the Soviet Union's nuclear armed ballistic missile complexes. Design of the R-5 was completed in October 1951, leading to a maiden launch on 15 March 1953, design work on the R-5M commencing that same year. Development of the R-5M had been authorised by a Soviet government decree issued on 19 April 1954. This missile complex, the maiden launch of which occurred on 21 January 1955, was capable of carrying a nuclear (special) warhead to a distance of 1200 km, bringing the weapon into the MRBM (Medium Range Ballistic Missile) category, which covered missiles with a firing range of 1111 km (600 nm) to 2778 km (1500 nm). As well as service use as a MRBM, a number of R-5 derivatives were developed as geophysical launch vehicles, including R-5A models, which were launched in the period 1958-1961, and the R-5B, examples of which were launched in the period 1964-1975 (Harkins, 2017 & Energia, 2016).

The R-5 MRBM (R-5M illustrated) was the first Soviet ballistic missile complex to be armed with a nuclear warhead. Energia

Although R-5 variants had been instrumental in bestowing upon the Soviet Union a nuclear armed ballistic missile capability, it was with the R-7 that the dawn of the ICBM and space travel would become a reality, this missile complex, at a stroke, catapulting the Soviet Union ahead of her competitors in both fields. The large R-7 had been developed under a Soviet government decree issued on 13 February 1953. This had called for development of what would become a two-stage missile of some 170 ton mass, incorporating a separating nose section containing a nuclear warhead of some 3000 kg mass – warhead specification changed in October 1953 to incorporate a fire charge mass of up to 3000 kg and total mass of up to 5500 kg. The R-7 could strike targets 8000 km distant from the launch site, taking it well beyond the 5556 km milestone that defined the ICBM category of ballistic missiles (Harkins, 2017).

The R-7, which entered service as an ICBM in August 1957, would lead to a whole family of space payload launch vehicles that included the Vostok and Molniya, which would lead to the Soyuz launch vehicle. The first ever payload delivery to Earth orbit was conducted on 4 November 1957, when a modified R-7 ICBM launched the world's first artificial satellite, Sputnik 1 (PS-1), setting the Soviet Union apart from the rest of the field in regards to development of space launch vehicles. This was the stone that started the ripple of shock waves that resonated around the world in the form of the *beep, beep, beep...* transmitted from the satellite back to Earth. The R-7 launch vehicle derivatives would be instrumental in the Soviet Union's capacity to maintain an undisputed lead in uninhabited and inhabited spaceflight for several years. Such launch vehicles proved to be suitable for near Earth orbit uninhabited and inhabited space flights, as well as several types of uninhabited Moon missions and interplanetary probes to Venus and Mars (Harkins, 2017).

The dawn of the age of space travel came with the launch of Sputnik 1 on a converted R-7 ICBM (R-7 ICBM illustrated) on 4 October 1957. This would lead to a plethora of Earth orbit, interplanetary and Moon craft, as well as the fractional orbit weapon system of the late 1960's. Energia

Whilst OKB-1 (separated from NII-88) certainly had the highest profile of the Soviet ballistic missile designers other design bureau were heavily involved in this field of development. In this regard, the fledgling NII-88 had forwarded to Vasily Budnik, Chief Designer at Dnepropetrovsk Factory No.586, plans and research data on what was referred to as a 'high boiling' missile on a par with the OKB-1 R-5. This early beginning would lead to the development and building of the prototype of the R-12 long-range ballistic missile under OKB-586, also referred to as SDB-586, as Factory No.586 had been renamed in 1954 (now Yuzhnoye State Design Office, Ukraine), headed by its chief designer, Mikhail Yangel. The first R-12 launch was conducted on 22 June 1957. This missile complex, with a maximum firing range of 2080 km, fell into the MRBM category (Harkins, 2017).

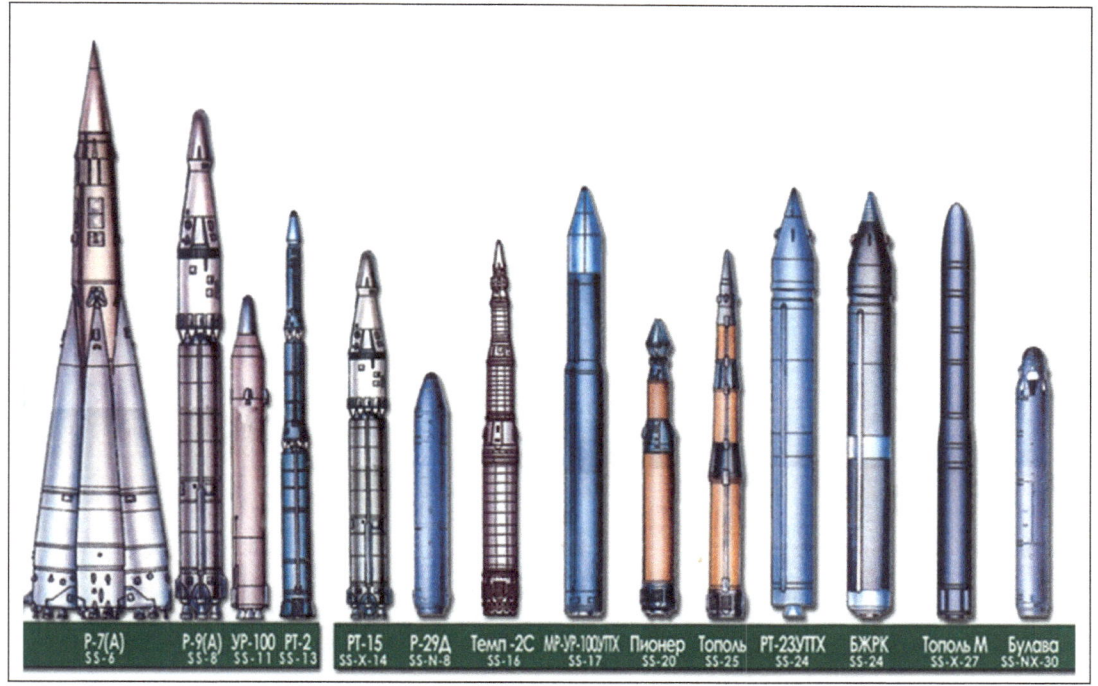

Partial evolution path of Soviet/Russian ICBM/SLBM/IRBM missile systems: R-7(A), R-9, UR-100, RT-2, RT-15, R-29, Temp-2C, PR-UR-100UTTX; Pioner (Pioneer); Topol; RT-23UTTX; БжРК; Topol M and Bulava. Academican Pilyugan Centre

Continued research and development would lead to the R-14, which, endowed with a maximum firing range of 4500 km, more than twice that of the R-12, fell into the IRBM (Intermediate Range Ballistic Missile) category that covered ranges from 2778 km up to 5556 km. This missile complex, the first launch of which was conducted in June 1960, featured increased accuracy over its forebears and the probability of instrumentation errors was reduced by the incorporation of a gyro-stabilised platform within the autonomous inertial control system. Further research and development led to the R-16, which, with a maximum firing range of 13000 km, was OKB-586's first ICBM to reach production status. Following redesign, to eliminate faults attributed to the cause of a launch pad explosion, an R-16 missile was successfully launched in February 1961, followed on 21 April that year by launch of the 13000 km range OKB-1 designed R-9 silo-based ICBM complex (operationally deployed from 21 July 1965) (Harkins, 2017).

Launch of an R-16 first generation Soviet silo based ICBM complex. YDB

While the R-12, R-14 and R-16 constituted the first generation of Soviet ballistic missile complexes developed by OKB-586, the bureaus next steps on the development ladder would lead to the R-36 and contributed to development of the UR-100 second generation ICBM complexes. These new systems, which would lead to a plethora of missile developments of third and fourth generations, inherited by the SMF of the Russian Federation and remaining in service in 2021, were spurred by the events of 1962. Having found herself at a major disadvantage in terms of strategic strike capability during the Cuban Missile Crisis of October 1962 (termed the 'Caribbean Crisis' in the Soviet Union and later Russian Federation), the Soviet leadership determined that such a situation was untenable. This resulted in a strategic armaments program of unprecedented scale, in which she intended to not only achieve parity with the United States, but overtake that nation to become the world's premier nuclear power in terms of both delivery vehicle numbers and throw weight/warhead yield. To this end, the Soviet ICBM force levels, along with other elements of her strategic strike forces, not least of which was a large SSBN (Nuclear Powered Ballistic Missile Submarine) build program, increased through the late 1960's and the 1970's. The latter decade would see the Soviet Union overtake the United States (the US ICBM force was predominantly focused on the lightweight silo based Minuteman variants with smaller numbers of Titan heavy ICBM's) in terms of numbers of deployed ballistic missile launchers available. The United States still had an advantage in its ability to target Soviet territory with MRBM and IRBM's, whereas the Soviets could not reciprocate in regards to the contiguous Continental United States (the American state of Alaska could be targeted by Soviet IRBM). The Soviet's did possess a large force of MRBM and IRBM's, the latter estimated at around 700 by the late 1960's, in which they could deploy extensively against targets in Eurasia (includes the United Kingdom) land mass in the event of conflict with NATO, and such missiles could have targeted other potential adversaries.

Launch of a UR-100 Soviet SMF second generation silo based ICBM. Krunichev

Experience gained in the development and operation of the Pioneer PGRK (mobile) intermediate range ballistic missile complex would later feed into the PGRK ICBM complexes of the fourth and fifth generations in service with the Russian SMF in the third decade of the twenty first century. Avangard

During the period 1965-1973, the SMF had put second generation ICBM complexes on combat alert as it built up parity with the USA in regard to nuclear strike potential. Between 1973 and 1985, the SMF placed third generation ICBM complexes on combat alert. These missile complexes were armed with multiple-warheads and incorporated aids to enhance the ability to penetrate potential missile defence systems. In addition to RS-18, RS-20 and RS-16 ICBM complexes, the Soviet Union introduced enhanced capability RSD-10 Pioneer mobile intermediate-range ballistic missile complexes that would pave the way for the future generation of advanced mobile ICBM complexes. The next phase of development, 1985 to 1992, saw the SMF adopt and place on combat alert a number of fourth generation silo based and mobile ICBM complexes, RS-22, RS-20V and Topol. Stepped modernisation also saw the introduction of a new automated fire control system for operation of ICBM complexes within the SMF (MODRF SMF, 2017).

The USSR was formally dissolved on 25 December 1991 and replaced by a Commonwealth of Independent States – former Soviet Republics. At that time, the SMF comprised six missile armies with 28 constituent missile divisions. Deployed Soviet ballistic missile numbers on combat alert had peaked in 1985 at around 2,500, including 1,398 ICBM's, the remainder made up of SLBM & IRBM etc., with deployed nuclear warheads numbers peaking at around 10,300 in 1986.

With the break-up of the Soviet Union there followed a decade of considerable upheaval and reorganisation – in 1992, the newly formed Russian Federation inherited the SMF organisation that carried the same function under the auspices of the now defunct USSR. At this stage, the SMF was formed as a service branch of the armed forces of the Russian Federation and the Russian Space Agency came into being on 25 February 1992 (MODRF Historical Archive for 25 February 1992).

The next decade and a half would be a period of underfunding and force reduction. Much of the missile armies constituent divisions/regiments were disbanded as the Russian Federation (which, as noted above, had emerged as the main USSR successor state) contracted her strategic forces. As well as the operational function of retaining nuclear deterrent ICBM divisions on combat alert, the SMF was heavily tasked with the deactivation and removal of former Soviet assets as missile complexes in former Soviet republics underwent gradual disbandment/relocation. This included missiles, missile launch facilities and warhead storage facilities located on the territory of the former Soviet Republics of the newly created Commonwealth of Independent States as the SMF concentrated all strategic missile assets within the borders of the Russian Federation. For example, the 33rd and 49th Missile Divisions, at Lida and Mozyr respectively on the soil of the Republic of Belorussia (now Belarus) commenced disbandment in 1995, the 32nd Missile Division having completed disbandment on 31 December 1993 (Vladimir Missile Association (Guards Missile Vitebsk Red Banner Army) History, MODRF, 2020).

The 1990's was also a period of ensuring the viability of the reduced nuclear deterrent forces, within a limited budget, through introduction of Topol-M fifth generation ICBM's (eventually introduced in silo and mobile based) under the command of General of the Army, Igor Dmitrievich Sergeev (later Minister of Defence of the Russian Federation). A significant change in the command structure of the SMF was implemented in 1997 with amalgamation of that organisation with the MS (Military Space Forces). In this regard, the SMF, commanded by General of the Army Vladimir Nikolavich Yakovlev, as well as commanding the extant missile armies and their constituent divisions, took on the function of spacecraft launch and control, previously associated with the SMF. Further administrative changes were implemented on 1 June 2001, on which date the SMF was removed from its position as a branch of the armed forces of the Russian Federation and re-established as two distinctly independent organisations – the Strategic Missile (Rocket) Forces (commanded by Colonel-General Nikolai Evgenievich Solovtsov, from 2001-2009) and the Space Forces – which would, nevertheless, retain close cooperation in their respective operations (MODRF).

From 2001-2009, the SMF continued force reductions in line with arms control treaty obligations and modernisation, within an environment of continuing budget constraints. For the short period of 2009 to June 2010, the SMF was under the command of Lieutenant General Andrei Anatolyevich Shvaichenko. During this period, increased funding allowed for a rise in the tempo of modernisation to increase the combat potential of the constituent missile divisions. In this regard, Topol-M missile complexes took up alert status with mobile missile regiments. Colonel-General Sergie Viktorovich Karakaev took over as commander of the SMF in June 2010. The next decade or so would be a period of intense activity in the two distinct realms of force reduction, to meet obligations agreed between the Russian

Federation and the US on implementation of the New START (Strategic Arms Limitation Treaty), effective from February 2011, and force modernisation, with the continued introduction of new missile systems and improvements to the deterrent effectiveness of existing systems. This latter area included introducing fifth generation Yars ICBM complexes and continued development of new generation strategic nuclear delivery systems that would emerge as the RS-28 Sarmat heavy ICBM complex and the Avangard hypersonic maneuverable glide vehicle, which would be carried into sub-orbit atop repurposed UR-100N UTTX ICBM's.

The RT-2PM Topol complex remained in operational service with a reducing number of units of the SMF going into 2021. These systems were progressively being replaced by Yars fifth generation ICBM complexes in SMF mobile regiments. In preparation for its imminent departure from service, this RT-2PM complex is prepared for display at the Suvorov School in Perm, Russia. MODRF

In 2021, the SMF included the command and control centres for three missile armies located in Vladimir, Omsk and Orengburg regions. The three missile armies maintained twelve missile division armed with six types of ICBM – silo based R-36M2 (RS-20V Voevoda) (silo), UR-100N UTTKh (UTTX) Stiletto (silo), RS-12M Topol (mobile), MS-12M2 (RT-2PM2) Topol-M (silo), 12M1-RS (RT-2PM1) Topol-M (mobile), RS-24 Yars (mobile), RS-24 Yars (silo) – in a state of combat alert for immediate response to a nuclear strike on the territory of the Russian Federation or one of her CSTO (Collective Security Treaty Organisation) member state allies.

2

NEW START AND THE RUSSIAN NUCLEAR POSTURE

The accelerating pace of strategic nuclear weapons deployment had indicated to the USSR (Union of Soviet Socialist Republics) and USA (United States of America) leaderships that a position of strategic parity would have to be accepted – a position that the Soviet Union had been vying for over a decade or so following the Caribbean Crisis of 1962 (Cuban Missile Crisis). This resulted in the formulation of the SALT (Strategic Arms Limitation Treaty) and START (Strategic Arms Reduction Treaty) as the main tools for governing arms control over the next several decades. In addition, other treaties, such as the ABM (Anti-Ballistic Missile) treaty of 1972 (the ABM Treaty was ratified in 1972 by the USA and USSR (later inherited by the Russian Federation) in conjunction with ratification of SALT on limiting the number of strategic nuclear weapons) and the INF (Intermediate range Nuclear Forces) treaty of 1987 (medium and intermediate range missiles, including RSD-10) expanded arms control mechanisms. The USA withdrawal from the ABM treaty in 2002 and the effective demise of the INF treaty (suspended by the United States in February 2019 and, in response, by Russia in March 2019) – (NATO clarified that it had no verifiable data on its claims that a Russian missile, 7M729, exceeded permitted range (NATO, 2019)) left only the New START (New Strategic Arms Reduction Treaty) to limit numbers of nuclear warheads and their delivery systems.

New START, remaining in force in 2021, superseded the START-1 arms limitation/reduction treaty, signed between the USSR and USA in Moscow on 3 July 1991 (MODRF Historical Archive, 3 July 1991). New START, which covered the further reduction and limitation of strategic nuclear weapons, signed by the Russian Federation and the USA, came into force on 15 February 2011, for a period of ten years, with the option for a further extension for a period of no more than five years. A key stipulation of the treaty was that both signatories reduced their strategic nuclear arsenals to no more than 700 deployed ICBM (Intercontinental Ballistic Missile), SLBM (Submarine Launched Ballistic Missile) and strategic bomber/missile carriers, and no more than 1,550 warheads deployed on these launch platforms – both parties could possess up to 800 ICBM, SLBM and strategic bomber/missile carriers, but only 700 could be operationally deployed.

Russia had expressed concern at rebuffs to a proposed extension to New START beyond the February 2021 expiration date (both parties entered into a five year extension in February 2021 – treaty set to expire in February 2026), this uncertainty was added to by NATO nation refusal to ratify the CTBT (Comprehensive Nuclear Test Ban Treaty) (Russia had ratified the CTBT administered by the CTBTO (Comprehensive Nuclear Test Ban Treaty Organisation), whilst the US, having failed to ratify the treaty, had observed a self-imposed moratorium on nuclear tests).

When discussing the Russian Federation nuclear triad it is pertinent to look at the nuclear posture of the Russian Federation and the USA (the United Kingdom and France have their own nuclear postures, but it is the USA posture that is pertinent in regard to a potential nuclear conflict between NATO and the Russian Federation). Whilst NATO had circulated contradictory documentation stating that as Russia lowers the threshold for nuclear weapons use the NATO alliance does not follow this path, a study of the nuclear postures of both parties provides clear evidence that the contrary is actually true. In addition, a situation of large-scale disinformation has emerged within much of the media of NATO nations aimed at painting the Russian Federation as an aggressor threatening to attack the NATO alliance with nuclear weapons. Among the tamer statements are along the lines of Russia planning to employ nuclear weapons as a tool of projecting terror and reserving the right to employ such weapons in regional conflicts. These fallacious statements, emanating from such publications as the Bulletin of Atomic Scientists, and apparently based on sources from media and NATO nations political/military, have no basis in fact and lack supporting evidence, being more in line with pushing geopolitics than providing an accurate appraisal of the Russian doctrine on the use of nuclear weapons. The Russian nuclear weapon employment doctrine is clear when reference is made to the only document that is relevant, the Russian Policy document, 'Basic Principals of State Policy of the Russian Federation on Nuclear Deterrence, 2020', which is omitted by NATO nation media and publications that push the fallacious Russian nuclear weapon employment doctrine narrative. This document emphatically states 'Russia views nuclear weapons exclusively as means of deterrence, and the use of which is an extreme forced measure'. Point 5 in Section I of the Policy document states unequivocally that 'The Russian Federation considers nuclear weapons exclusively as a means of deterrence, their use being an extreme and compelled measure, and takes all necessary efforts to reduce nuclear threats and prevent aggravation of interstate relations, that could trigger military conflicts, including nuclear ones' (Basic Principals of State Policy of the Russian Federation on Nuclear Deterrence, 2020). Point 9 in Section II states 'Nuclear deterrence is aimed to provide comprehension by a potential adversary of the inevitability of retaliation in the event of aggression against the Russian Federation and/or its allies' (Basic Principals of State Policy of the Russian Federation on Nuclear Deterrence, 2020). Point 19 of Section III, 'Conditions for the transition of the Russian Federation to the use of nuclear weapons' states:

> "The conditions specifying the possibility of nuclear weapons use by the Russian Federation are as follows: a) arrival of reliable data on a launch of ballistic missiles

attacking the territory of the Russian Federation and/or its allies; b) use of nuclear weapons or other types of weapons of mass destruction by an adversary against the Russian Federation and/or its allies; c) attack by [an] adversary against critical government or military sites of the Russian Federation, disruption of which would undermine nuclear forces response actions; d) aggression against the Russian Federation with the use of conventional weapons when the very existence of the state is in jeopardy" (Basic Principals of State Policy of the Russian Federation on Nuclear Deterrence, 2020).

As can be determined from this document, the current (2020, effective in 2021) Russian Federation nuclear posture envisages that one of two thresholds would have to be crossed before a nuclear strike can be authorised: 1. When Russia or one of her allies [CSTO (Collective Security Treaty Organisation) states] has been attacked with nuclear weapons. 2. When the very existence of the Russian Federation as a sovereign nation is threatened. This latter point includes an attack by conventional weapons designed to destroy or degrade the potential for Russia to retaliate against a nuclear strike. From a Russian standpoint, this would include attacks against the political/military higher command in an attempt to remove the ability for a nuclear retaliatory strike to be ordered, or attacks against nuclear strike assets, again, to erode the potential for a retaliatory Russian nuclear response to a follow up nuclear attack, or a conventional attack against the Russian missile warning assets (ground based or space based), which would be considered a precursor to an adversary nuclear attack on the Russian Federation through removing her ability to detect and track ballistic missile launches and incoming warheads. In short, conventional attacks on infrastructure essential for the Russian Federation to respond to a nuclear attack would be considered a precursor for a nuclear strike against Russia, inviting a full retaliatory nuclear response – the very essence of deterrence.

Whilst a cursory study of the Russian Federation policy document on the employment of nuclear weapons clearly demonstrates advocating of a last resort use of nuclear weapons, by contrast, the NATO alliance, in the 2010's has fostered plans to move forward with a doctrine that lowers the threshold for a nuclear strike on an adversary. The February 2018 NPR (Nuclear Posture Review) appears to suggest that the US would employ nuclear weapons against an adversary that had employed conventional weapons against the US or one of her allies (it is unclear if this would be a conventional attack against infrastructure critical to the US ability to conduct a retaliatory nuclear strike response to a follow-up nuclear strike). Furthermore, the 2018 NPR places greater emphasis on the use of nuclear weapons compared to the 2010 NPR. The 2018 NPR goes further by embracing the concept of limited nuclear exchanges, a posture pondered and abandoned as unsound during the high threat days of the late Cold War era. This limited nuclear exchange concept of war was rejected by the Russian Federation, which advocated that nuclear weapon use is a last resort and that even a limited nuclear strike on Russia or one of her allies would invite a full retaliatory response from that nation's nuclear deterrent triad. In short, the use of nuclear weapons, even on a limited scale, against the territory of the Russian Federation or her allies would be met with a large-scale nuclear strike against the perpetrator state(s) – the true essence of a deterrent – to attempt to kill the

Russian Federation as a state would also become an aggressors suicide in line with the late Cold War concept of MAD (Mutually Assured Destruction).

Following the US withdrawal from the ABM treaty in 2002, the Russian Federation ramped up development work on advanced strategic strike systems to nullify the then planned NATO missile defence shield, which threatened to degrade Russia's nuclear deterrent potential. Development and introduction of new advanced weapon systems able to counter NATO attempts to nullify Russia's nuclear deterrent force potential may be viewed as a two pronged spear. If the US had opted to let New START expire (as noted above, this treaty was extended for a period five years, effective from February 2021) then the new Russian strategic weapon systems would ensure her security against what it perceived as an aggressive NATO alliance with territorial ambitions against the Russian Federation and her allies (several NATO member and NATO partner nations have pushed unsound territorial claims against the Russian Federation or her allies/protectorates), even in a climate of increased strategic weapon deployment by NATO. The new strategic strike systems, it was hoped, would provide the Russian Federation with the strategic strike currency it required to convince the NATO (principally United States) political leadership to embrace the pragmatism of their forebears and accept the late Cold War era principle that neither side could win a nuclear war and that such a course of action should, therefore, be avoided at all costs through the extension of the New START arms control mechanism, now set to expire in February 2026.

The precise figures for strategic strike systems operational under the terms of the New START Treaty at 1 March 2021 were published by the Russian Federation government in May 2021. The document indicated that Russia had 517 operational strategic strike systems, comprised of ICBM, SLBM and strategic missile carrier aircraft, with 1,456 nuclear warheads deployed on those platforms. The document indicated that the United States had 651 operational strategic strike systems – ICBM, SLBM and heavy bomber/missile carrier aircraft, with 1,357 warheads deployed on these platforms. The revealed data confirmed that whilst the US retained a higher number of operational delivery systems, the Russian Federation retained a higher number of operational warheads on its delivery systems. The values for total numbers of operational and non-operational ICBM, SLBM launchers and long-range strategic missile carrier/bomber aircraft are 767 for the Russian Federation and 800 for the United States (Notifications under Provision 2, Section II, Part 4 of the New START agreement, 2021). It was noted that the United States value of 800 launchers was achieved through omission of 56 Trident II SLBM and 41 Boeing B-52H heavy bomber/missile carrier aircraft, the Russian Federation raising the point that it had not been satisfactorily verified that these systems had been modified to a stage where they could not be employed as nuclear warhead delivery systems. In addition, four facilities for strategic ballistic missile launch were declared by the United States as training facilities rather than listed under the non-operational missile launchers. As at May 2021, these points had been raised by the Russian Federation as the United States having exceeded the permitted number of missile launchers under Provision 1c, Article II of New START.

3

MISSILE ARMIES AND MISSILE DIVISIONS OF THE STRATEGIC MISSILE FORCES

In 2021, the Russian SMF (Strategic Missile Forces) missile armaments were organised into three missile armies under the overall command of Karakayev Sergey Viktorovich, whom assumed the position under direction of a Presidential decree dated 22 June 2010. He had previously held several posts within the organisation – commander of the Vladimir missile connection, from 2006-2008 and Chief of Staff First Deputy Commander of the SMF, from October 2009 (MODRF, 2017).

The three Missile Armies consisted of the Vladimir Missile Association (Guards Missile Vitebsk Red Banner Army), the Orenburg Missile Association (Orenburg Missile Army) and the Omsk Missile Association (Guards Missile Berislav Khingan, twice Red Banner Order of Suvorov Army). There were twelve separate missile connections (divisions) associated with the three missile armies: Bologove Missile Formation (Rezhitsa Red Banner Guards Missile Division) – also referred to as Bologoevskoe missile compound (Guards Krasnoznamennaya Rezhitskaya missile division); Barnaul Missile Formation (Red Banner Orders of Kutuzov and Aleksandr (Aleksandra) Nevsky Missile Division) – also referred to as Barnaul missile compound (rocket Krasnoznamennaya orders Kutuzov and Aleksandra Nevskogo Division); Irkutsk Missile Formation (Vitebsk Guards Red Banner Order of Lenin Missile Division) – also referred to as Irkutskoye missile compound (Guards missile Vitebsk Lenin Krasnoznamennaya Division); Yoshkar-Ola Missile Formation (Kiev-Zhitomir Order of Kutuzov 3rd Grade Missile Division); Kozelsk (Kozelskoye) Missile Formation (Red Banner (Guards Krasnoznamennaya) Guards Missile Division); Novosibirsk Missile Formation (Glukhov Red Banner Orders of Lenin, Suvorov, Kutuzov and B. Khmel'nitsky Guards Missile Division) (also referred to as Guards Gluhovskaya Lenin, Krasnoznamennaya orders Suvorov Kutuzov and B. Khmel'nickogo Missile Division); Tarishchevo Missile Formation (Tatischev (Tatishevsky) Missile Connection) (Taman Red Banner Order of October Revolution (Krasnoznamennaya) Missile Division); Tagil (Tagilshoye) Missile Formation (Tagil (Tagilshoye) Missile Division); Teykovo (Teikov/Teykovsky) Missile Formation

(Order of Kutuzov Guards Missile Division); Uzhur Missile Formation (Red Banner Missile Division) – also referred to as Uzhurskogo missile compound (Krasnoznamennaya Missile Division); Yurya Missile Formation (Melitopol Red Banner Missile Division) (also referred to as the Yuranskoye Missile Compound (Melitopol Krasnoznamennaya Missile Division) or Yuryansky missile unit (Melitopol Red Banner Missile Division); Yasny Missile Formation (Red Banner Missile Division) – also referred to as Yasnenskoe missile compound (Missile Krasnoznamennaya Division) and a connection of the State Central Multipurpose Firing Range of the Russian Federation Ministry of Defence. The divisions incorporated constituent regiments, numbering in the region of 39, notwithstanding stand-down, stand-up periods.

MISSILE ARMIES – *Vladimir Missile Association (Vitebsk Red Banner Guards Missile Army)* – The Vladimir Missile (Rocket) Association (Guards Missile Vitebsk Red Banner Army) lineage, in regard to the SMF, dated back to the 1960 formation of three missile brigades from the 46th Artillery Range (educational formation) and the 7th Guards Cannon Artillery Vitebsk Red Banner Division RVGK. The organisation of these formations were reformed into the Guard Missile Vitebsk Red Banner Army in 1970. Through the 1970's and into the 1980's, the constituent divisions (formations underwent changes and the Guards Missile Rezhitskaya Division was transferred to the control of the 50th Missile Army (Smolensk) were it was armed with a plethora of missile systems – R-16, RS-10, SD-100, RSD-10 – and moved from single warhead to MRV (Multiple Reentry Vehicle) and MIRV (Multiple Independently targetable Reentry Vehicle). It was in the 1980's that significant enhancements to the mobile missile capability of the SMF was realised through modernisation of ground mobile systems in the Teikov and Yoshkar-Ola divisions, which were equipped with PGRK (mobile strategic missile complex) Poplar. In July 1983, the Soviet Union stole a march on its western adversary with the formation of a BZHRK (rail mobile ICBM (Intercontinental Ballistic Missile)) regiment (commanded by Colonel S.D. Gorbatyuk) equipped with the 15P961 missile complex of the RT-23 Molodets (RS-22) (Vladimir Missile Association (Guards Missile Vitebsk Red Banner Army History, 2017), whilst that planned in the US (United States) fell by the wayside

The missile army underwent further organisational changes to become the Guards Missile Vitebsk Red Banner Army (Missile Army) in January 1984. Through the 1980's, RT-2PM (RS-12M) Topol ICBM complexes were progressively introduced, the first such regiment (commanded by Lieutenant Colonel V.V. Dremova) assuming combat alert on 23 July 1985. The 15P961 missile of the RT-23 (RS-22) BZHRK was placed on combat alert with the Tatischev formation in 1989. On 30 June 1990, the formations of the 50th Missile Army (Smolensk) – RS-16A/RS-16B etc. – was absorbed by the Guards Missile Rezhitskaya Red Banner Division (Vypolzovo). This brought the number of missile types in service with the Missile Army in 1990 to five – RS-18, RS-16A/B, RS-12M (Topol), RS-22 (BZHRK) and RS-22 (silo launched 15P060 missile complex). Mobile Topol missile complexes of what would become the Vladimir Missile Association (Guards Missile Vitebsk Red Banner Army) participated in the Parade in Red Square, Moscow, on 7 November 1990 (Vladimir Missile Association (Guards Missile Vitebsk Red Banner Army) History, 2017).

Following the upheavals and financial constraints placed on the SMF in the immediate post-Soviet period, the Missile Division located at the village of Tatischev (Tatischevo) placed on experimental combat duty the RS-12M2 (RT-2PM2) Topol-M on 25 December 1997 – Topol-M attained permanent combat alert status on 28 April 2000. A Further RT-2PM2 missile unit (silo based) was established at Tatischevo on 30 December 1998 (Vladimir Missile Association (Guards Missile Vitebsk Red Banner Army) History, 2017).

Page 18: RS-24 Yars ICBM en-route from Teikov to a temporary basing location at Alabino, Moscow, on 26 February 2019. Page 19: Mobile ICBM complexes of the 480th regiment, 35th missile division on deployment. MODRF

In July 2002, the Vladimir Missile Army took on some of the combat strength of the Orenburg Missile Army – RS-12M (RT-2PM) missiles of the Kiev-Zhitomir Division Orders of Kutuzov (Yoshkar-Ola). By 1 December 2005, the 10th Missile Division H.Q (Headquarters), located at Kostroma, Russia, formally completed disbandment. This paved the way for the reformation of the missile division (H.Q. located at Teikov armed with PGRK (mobile) Topol-M ICBM, in 2006. This division was subsequently armed with PGRK Yars in 2010 (Vladimir Missile Association (Guards Missile Vitebsk Red Banner Army) History, 2020).

Toward the close of the second decade of the twenty first century, the Vladimir Missile Association (Guards Missile Vitebsk Red Banner Army) constituent units were on combat alert with RS-12M (Topol), RS-12M2 (Topol-M) (mobile and silo based), RS-24 (Yars) and RS-18 (Vladimir Missile Association (Guards Missile Vitebsk Red Banner Army) History, 2020).

Orenburg Missile Association (Orenburg Missile Army) – Under a directive issued by the then commander of the Soviet Strategic Missile Force, what, in 2021, was the Orenburg Missile Association (Orenburg Missile Army) was initially formed on the basis of the 18th Separate Missile Body, on 7 July 1965 (commanded by Major General of Aviation, G.P. Brown). This organisation would constitute a Corp with three missile divisions, controlled by the 18th Separate Missile Body from 6 September 1965. The missile body was placed on combat alert under the auspices of the Orenburg Missile Body on 27 November 1966. It was further organised into a Missile Army from March 1970, and, in June that year, it was established as a Missile Army within the SMF, with H.Q. located at Orenburg (commanded by Hero of the Soviet Union, Lieutenant-General I.A. Shevtsov). In 2020, the Orenburg Missile Association (Orenburg Missile Army) comprised three missile divisions headquartered at Yurya, Nizhniy and Tagil respectively, armed with RS-12M Poplar and RS-20V (R-36M2) Voevoda ICBM complexes (Orenburg Missile Association (Orenburg Missile Army History, 2020).

Omsk Missile Association (Berislav-Khingan, Twice Red Banner Order of Suvarov Guards Missile Army) – The unit (organisational) that would become the Omsk Missile Association (Guards Missile Berislav Khingan, twice Red Banner Order of Suvarov Army) was formed from the 109th Guards Rifle Division on 1 September 1959. This was initially on the basis of an artillery (missile) training formation, which took on the organisation and function of a Separate Missile Corp from 10 March 1961, before its metamorphous into a Guards Missile Army near the city of Omsk on 23 April 1970 (Omsk Missile Association (Omsk Missile Association (Berislav-Khingan, Twice Red Banner Order of Suvarov Guards Missile Army) History, 2020).

In 2020, the major unit establishments of the Missile Army consisted of: Novosibirsk Missile Formation (Glukhov Red Banner Orders of Lenin, Suvorov, Kutuzov and B. Khmel'nitsky Guards Missile Division); Barnaul Missile Formation (Red Banner Orders of Kutuzov and Aleksandr (Aleksandra) Nevsky Missile Division) and Irkutsk Missile Formation (Vitebsk Guards Red Banner Orders of Lenin Missile Division). The ICBM complexes of the Army's constituent divisions consisted of RS-12M and RS-20V Voevoda (Omsk Missile Association (Berislav-Khingan, Twice Red Banner Order of Suvarov Guards Missile Army) History, 2020).

Yars and Topol PGRK mobile missile divisions conducted combat patrols on remote routes in the full-range of environmental conditions found in Russia's vast expanse, including extreme winter snowfalls. MODRF

MISSILE DIVISIONS – (1) *Bologove Missile Formation (Rezhitsa Red Banner Guards Missile Division)* – What would become the Bologove (Bologoevskoe) Missile Formation (Krasnoznamennaya) (Rezhitsa Red Banner Guards Missile Division) was formed as a missile brigade from the 19 Pabr Brigade, which had formed on 14 July 1943 as the 19th Cannon-Artillery Brigade (Pabr), itself formed from the 79th Guards Cannon-Artillery Regiment. In April 1961, the brigade was brought to Division strength, taking on the title Guards Missile Rezhitsa Division. As work continued toward an operational status, the Division was placed on combat alert armed with the R-5 IRBM (Intermediate Range Ballistic Missile) on 11 February 1963, the first training launch of this missile complex under the divisional command structure being conducted by Military Unit 14264. During the course of several decades the missile division was armed with several ICBM complexes: UR-100, from 1967, RS-16A, from 1975 and RS-16B, from 1979. The division, now holding the name Guards Krasnoznamennaya Rezhitsa Missile Division, headquartered at the Bologoevskoe missile compound, received RT-2PM (RS-12M) Topol missile systems in 1994, and one of the divisions constituent regiments was allocated the honorary name 'Tverskoy' by a decree of the President of the Russian Federation of 27 November 1999 (Bologove Missile Formation (Rezhitsa Red Banner Guards Missile Division History, 2020).

Page 22-23: RT-2PM Topol PGRK 15U168 transport launch vehicles and engineering vehicles of a SMF missile regiment in the Tver region, a constituent unit of the Bologove Missile Formation (Rezhitsa Red Banner Guards Missile Division), are secured at their temporary field deployment during a training exercise. MODRF

Transport launch vehicle and accommodation vehicle from a Bologove Missile Formation (Rezhitsa Red Banner Guards Missile Division) ICBM regiment. MODRF

(2) *Barnaul Missile Formation (Red Banner Orders of Kutuzov and Aleksandr (Aleksandra) Nevsky Missile Division)* – The formation that would become the Barnaul Missile Formation (Red Banner Orders of Kutuzov and Aleksandr (Aleksandra) Nevsky Missile Division) (also referred to as the Rocket Krasnoznamennaya Orders Kutuzov and Aleksandra Nevsky (Nevskogo) Division) was formed as the 46th Rocket (Missile) Brigade under an order issued by the Minister of Defence of the USSR (Union of Soviet Socialist Republics). This brigade, which absorbed the 65th heavy mortar Red Orders of Kutuzov and Aleksandra Brigade and a brigade of the 6th Artillery Division, formulated as a missile division by an order of the Minister of Defence of the USSR, dated April 1961. Following several moves, divisional headquarters settled near the village of Borovikha, Altai Territory (Barnaul Missile Formation (Red Banner Orders of Kutuzov and Aleksandra Nevsky Missile Division) History, 2020).

In the second decade of the twenty first century, missile formations equipped with RT-2PM Topol were progressively rearmed with RS-24 Yars – one such complex here on combat patrol, circa 22 June 2019. MODRF

The missile division commenced combat alert with the RT-2PM Topol ICBM complex at the Barnaul missile compound in 1983. This missile formation had previously operated R-12 IRBM from 1961-1981 and R-14 ICBM missiles from 1963-1982 (Barnaul Missile Formation (Red Banner Orders of Kutuzov and Aleksandra Nevsky Missile Division) History, 2020).

(3) *Irkutsk Missile Formation (Vitebsk Guards Red Banner Order of Lenin Missile Division)* – What in 2020 constituted the Irkutsk Missile Formation (Vitebsk Guards Red Banner Orders of Lenin Missile Division) was formed from the 51st Guards Rifle Vitebsk Orders of Lenin Red Banner Division, entering combat alert as a SMF

missile division on 4 June 1960. One of the constituent regiments, armed with R-12 IRBM, was deployed to Cuba under operation Anadyr from July-December 1962 – being at the centre of the Caribbean Crisis/Cuban Missile Crisis. Toward the end of the second decade of the twenty first century, the division was armed with RT-2PM (RS-12M) Topol mobile ICBM (Irkutsk Missile Formation (Vitebsk Guards Red Banner Order of Lenin Missile Division) History, 2020). A MODRF release dated 11.09.2017 confirmed that personnel from the Irkutsk missile connection were undergoing training at the Plesetsk space centre (cosmodrome), Arkhangelsk region on the RS-24 Yars PGRK (mobile ICBM) complex, which was replacing the PGRK Topol then on combat alert (Department of Mass Communications of the Russian Federation Ministry of Defence, 2017).

RT-2PM (RS-12M) Topol mobile ICBM complex of the Yoshkar-Ola Missile Formation (Kiev-Zhitomir Orders of Kutuzov 3rd Grade Missile Division. MODRF

(4) *Yoshkar-Ola Missile Formation (Kiev-Zhitomir Orders of Kutuzov 3rd Grade Missile Division)* – The Yoshkar-Ola missile Formation (Kiev-Zhitomir Orders of Kutuzov 3rd (III) Division) lineage can be traced back to the 222nd ITAP (Fighter Anti-Tank Artillery Regiment), which was formed on 1 February 1942, and subsequently thrown into the Soviet effort to combat German forces facing Moscow during the first winter of the German invasion. Its association as a missile formation began on 25 May 1960 when the 201st Missile Brigade was instituted, the formation becoming a missile division at Yoshkar-Ola. The 201st Missile Division was formally allocated the title 'Kiev-Zhitomir Orders of Kutuzov III Division on 17 April 1967. Over the

course of several decades the division was armed with several missile complexes: R-16U, from 1969-1977; RT-2, from 1971-1980 and RT-2PM Topol, from 1976-1994 (1995). A regiment of the division was placed on combat alert with Topol at the Yoshkar-Ola site on 23 July 1985. The RT-2PM2 (RS-12M) was placed on combat alert with the division from 1995, this missile complex remaining in service with the division at the close of the second decade of the twenty first century (Yoshkar-Ola missile compound (Yoshkar-Ola Missile Formation (Yoshkar-Ola Missile Formation (Kiev-Zhitomir Orders of Kutuzov 3rd Grade Missile Division History, 2020).

Empty silo awaiting occupancy of a UR-100N UTTX ICBM of the Kozelsk (Kozelskoye) Missile Formation (Red Banner Guards Missile Division). MODRF

(5) *Kozelsk (Kozelskoye) Missile Formation (Red Banner (Guards Krasnoznamennaya) Guards Missile Division)* – The entity that constituted the Kozelsk (Kozelskoye) Missile Formation (Red Banner (Guards Krasnoznamennaya) Guards Missile Division) in 2021 was initially formed on 3 May 1961 from the 198th Missile Brigade, itself formed from the 28th Guards Cannon-Artillery Red Banner Brigade in June 1960. Over the course of several decades, the Division was armed with a number of ICBM complexes: R-9A, from 1964-1976; UR-100, from 1967-1977; UR-100N, from 1975-1987 and UR-100N UTTX from 1982 – the Kozelsk missile compound began replacing UR-100N with updated UR-100N UTTX in 1982, this missile complex remaining extant in 2021 (Kozelsk Missile Formation (Red Banner Guards Missile Division) History, 2020).

Winter conditions training with Glukhov Red Banner Orders of Lenin, Suvorov, Kutuzov and B. Khmel'nitsky Guards Missile Division RT-2PM Transport Launch Vehicle (top) and convoy protection forces (bottom). MODRF

(6) *Novosibirsk Missile Formation (Glukhov Red Banner Orders of Lenin, Suvorov, Kutuzov and B. Khmel'nitsky Guards Missile Division)* (also referred to as Guards Gluhovskaya Lenin, Krasnoznamennaya Orders Suvorov Kutuzov and B. Khmel'nickogo Missile Division) – On 11 June 1961, wat would become the Novosibirsk Missile Formation (Glukhov Red Banner Orders of Lenin, Suvorov, Kutuzov and B. Khmel'nitsky Guards Missile Division) was formed from the Guards Glukhov Orders of Lenin Red Banner Orders of Suvorov, Kutuzov and B. (Bogdan) Khmel'nitsky artillery division. The division was armed with R-16 ICBM's from 1963-1979 and RSD-10 IRBM at the Novosibirsk missile compound, from 1977-1989 (eliminated under the terms of the INF (Intermediate range Nuclear Forces Treaty) and RT-2PM (RS-12M) (Topol) ICBM from 1989, this latter missile complex remaining in service in 2020 (Novosibirsk Missile Formation (Glukhov Red Banner Orders of Lenin, Suvorov, Kutuzov and B. Khmel'nitsky Guards Missile Division) History, 2020).

RT-2PM mobile ICBM complex of a regiment of the Novosibirsk Missile Formation on a combat patrol route in severe Russian winter conditions. Conflicting data attached to the image states that the patrol is in the Tver Region of Russia. MODRF

(7) *Tarishchevo Missile Formation (Tatischev Missile Connection) (Taman Red Banner Orders of October Revolution Missile Division)* – The Tarishchevo Missile Formation (Tatischev Missile Connection) (Taman Red Banner Orders of October Revolution Missile Division) was initially formed on 28 May 1961 as the Taman Red Banner Rocket Division from the 229th Fighter Aviation Taman Red Banner Division. The newly established missile division was incorporated into the Soviet 9th Separate Missile

Corp. A nucleus of the division was placed on combat alert with two R-12 IRBM launchers on 15 January 1962. Elements of the division took part in operation Anadyr, placing R-12 missiles systems on combat alert in Cuba from 11 September until 20 November 1962. The division was incorporated into the 5th Kirov Separate Missile Corp (OPK) at Tatishchevo, Saratov region by 14 July 1964, for subsequent arming with second generation ICBM's of the UR-100 complex (silo based), all of the divisions' constituent regiments being armed and placed on combat alert with this missile complex by 12 August 1968. The missile division, which, on 17 December 1982, was formally named Taman missile Orders of the October Revolution Red Banner Division (Taman Red Banner Orders of October Revolution Missile Division), operated several missile complexes over several decades. In regard to ICBM's, this consisted of UR-100 (noted above) from 1966-1978; UR-100N, from 1976-1984; UR-100N UTTX, from 1982 (progressively retired in the 2010's); RT-23UTTX from 1989 (retired under arms control measures – START (Strategic Arms Reduction Treaty) – and RT-2PM2 (RS-12M2) silo based ICBM complexes from 1997 (extant in 2020) (Tarishchevo Missile Formation (Tatischev Missile Connection) (Taman Red Banner Orders of October Revolution Missile Division) History, 2020).

Equipment convoy belonging to a missile regiment of the Tatischev Missile Connection) (Taman Red Banner Orders of October Revolution Missile Division) proceeds to a base location in winter conditions of snow and ice. The missile division maintained constituent regiments on combat alert year round. MODRF

Test launches of Topol-M and Yars ICBM complexes were conducted along similar lines. MODRF

(8) *Tagil (Tagilshoye) Missile Formation (Tagil Missile Division)* – In the period 11 June to 1 December 1960, the entity of that would become the Tagil Missile Formation (Tagil Missile Division) was initially formed as the Soviet 202nd Missile Brigade from the 19th Howitzer Artillery Brigade, Carpathian Military District, and the 19th Training Tank Regiment of the Ural Military District. The missile brigade was formally established as a missile division by an order of the General Staff of the SMF (RVSN), dated 13 April 1961. Over the course of six decades, the division was armed with several missile complexes: R-16U, from 1960-1977, RSD-10, from 1978-1985 and RT-2PM (Topol), from 1986, this latter missile complex remaining in service in 2020 (*Tagil Missile Formation (Tagil Missile Division)* History, 2020).

(9) *Teykovo (Teikov) Missile Formation (Orders of Kutuzov Guards Missile Division)* – The formation that would become the Teykovo (Teikov) Missile Formation (Orders of Kutuzov Guards Missile Division) also referred to as the Teykovo (Teikov) missile formation (Guards missile Orders of the Kutuzov Division) was initially formed, under a directive of the Minister of Defence of the USSR of May 1960, as the Soviet 197th Missile Brigade from the 27th Guards Gun Artillery Order of Kutuzov, the Brigade of 7th Cannon-Artillery Division, the 541st Artillery Regiment and the 207th School of Mechanics. In April 1961, the USSR Minister for Defence authorised that the missile brigade would take on the mantle of a missile division designated as the Guards Missile Orders of Kutuzov II class Division, with its headquarters at the city of Teykovo (Teikov). Over a period of six decades, the division was armed with several missile complexes: R-16U, from 1962-1977; UR-100, from 1968-1975; UR-100K, from 1971-1991; RT-2PM, from 1988-2009; RT-2PM2, from 2006 and RS-24 Yars, from 2010 – the RT-2PM2 and RS-24 constituted the divisions ICBM armament in 2020 (Teykovo (Teikov) Missile Formation (Orders of Kutuzov Guards Missile Division) History, 2020).

Mobile ICBM transport launch vehicles of the Teikov Missile Formation (Orders of Kutuzov Guards Missile Division. MODRF

In 2020, the constituent missile regiments of the Teykovo (Teikov) Missile Formation (Orders of Kutuzov Guards Missile Division) were armed with Topol-M and RS-24 Yars ICBM complexes. Page 33-35 various ICBM Transport Launch Vehicle and associated engineering and armored personnel carrier/anti-sabotage vehicles of the mobile missile regiments of the division. MODRF

(10) *Uzhur Missile Formation (Red Banner Missile Division)* – The entity that would constitute the Uzhur Missile Formation (Red Banner Missile Division) (some English translation from Russian documents refer to this entity as the Uzhurskogo missile compound (Krasnoznamennaya Missile Division) in 2020 can trace its lineage back to the Soviet 109th Guards Rifle Division, from which a missile regiment was formed on 1 November 1960. The regiment was formed into a *bona fide* Missile Division (termed Military Unit 54093) in May 1964, with temporary deployment in Tomsk, Pyotr Mikhailovich Prikhodko, taking up formal duties as the first commander of the newly established missile division on 8 September that year. On 1 December 1964, the division was established at a permanent deployment area in Uzhur, Krasnoyarsk Territory. During the course of almost six decades, the missile division was armed with several ICBM complexes: R-36, from 1966-1979; R-36M, from 1975-1992; R-36M UTTX, from 1979-2008 and R-36M2 Voevoda, from 1992 – this later missile complex remained in service with the division in 2020 (Uzhur Missile Formation (Red Banner Missile Division) History, 2020).

Loading a missile of an R-36M2 heavy ICBM complex of the Uzhur Missile Formation (Red Banner Missile Division) into a SMF silo. MODRF

(11) The *Yurya Missile Formation (Melitopol Red Banner Missile Division)* (also referred to as the Yuranskoye (Yuryanskoe) Missile Compound (Melitopol Krasnoznamennaya Missile Division) or Yuryansky missile unit (Melitopol Red Banner Missile Division) was formed, on 12 November 1962, from the 91st Infantry Division, Orders of the Red Banner Melitopol (previously the 91st Melitopol Red Banner Rifle Division). Over the course of six decades the division was armed with several missile complexes, including the R-16, from 1961-1977 and RSD-10, from 1978 until 1985. In 1993, the division was incorporated into the Orenburg Missile Army of the SMF (Yurya Missile Formation (Melitopol Red Banner Missile Division) History, 2020).

(12) Yasny Missile Formation (Red Banner Missile Division) – What today constitutes the Yasny Missile Formation (Red Banner Missile Division), also referred to as the Yasnenskoe missile compound (rocket Krasnoznamennaya Division) was formed as a missile division in February 1965. Under a decree of the Presidium of the Supreme Soviet of the USSR the division was allocated Red Banner status on 22 February 1968. Over the course of several decades the division changed titles and operated various modifications of the R-36: R-36, from 1966-1978; R-36M, from 1974-1984; R-36M UTTX, from 1979-2009 and R-36M2 (RS-20V) Voevoda, from 1998 (Yasny Missile Formation (Red Banner Missile Division) History, 2020). This latter missile complex remained in service in 2021.

Launch (01.08 am on 26 March 2015) of an R-36M2 (RS-20V) silo based heavy ICBM in the Orenburg region of Russia. This was conducted under the auspices of the conversion program, whereby missiles that had reached the limit of their service lives were disposed of through launch. MODRF

Kapustin Yar – Another organisational entity that has to be considered in any appraisal of the SMF is the 4th State Central Interspecific Range of the Ministry of Defence of the Russian Federation (the Kapustin Yar test site), which comes under the authority of the command structure of the SMF, although it is also utilised by other branches of the Russian armed forces. The operational equipment incorporated into ICBM complexes is tested at Kapustin Yar, which is equipped with an extensive complex of sensors to track the delivery of ICBM payloads from launch site to the target range. Although specifically the domain of the MODRF, the Kapustin Yar range is integrated into the Russian military industrial complex in line with its role of testing new equipment under development (Kapustin Yar History, 2020).

In addition to trials at Kapustin Yar, the SMF regularly conducted ICBM test launches from the Plesetsk cosmodrome, Russia, although this site was not administered under the SMF command structure. The Plesetsk Cosmodrome test centre came under administrative control of the 15th Army of the Aerospace Forces (Special Purpose), itself under the control of the Main Centre for Exploration of Space. This latter unit monitored the space environment of spacecraft, ballistic missiles, space junk and natural celestial object threats. Typical of the work of the centre was the following: Over several months in 2017 the centre located around 1,000 near space objects, monitored the entry into Earth dense atmospheric layers of 190 objects, provided monitoring data on the insertion of in excess of 350 spacecraft (satellites etc.) into Earth orbit, provided warnings of proximity threats of objects with Russian satellites and, in cooperation with other elements of the missile warning system, in excess of 50 ballistic missile and space payload launches, domestic Russian and foreign, were noted (MODRF, 10.04, 2017).

ICBM complexes were tested at a number of centres, including the 4th State Central Interspecific Range of the Ministry of Defence of the Russian Federation, the Kapustin Yar test site. MODRF

Through the 2010's, RS-24 Yars mobile ICBM complexes (top) progressively replaced older generations systems of the RT-2PM Topol (bottom), a transport launch vehicle of the Barnaul Missile Connection illustrated. MODRF

RS-24 simulator complex (top) and engineering bench stand (bottom) of the 161st (161-I) Strategic Missile Force Technicians School (Astrakhan Region). MODRF

Practical training with the 161st (161-I) Strategic Missile Force Technicians School (Astrakhan Region). MODRF

Training and Miscellaneous Organisations – In addition to the missile armies and their subordinate units there were, in 2021, three major training centres and technical schools within the organisation of the SMF: The *161st (161-I) Strategic Missile Force Technicians School* (Astrakhan Region) – training on various technical equipment, including the plethora of vehicles (including MAZ-7917 and MAZ-543) operated by the SMF mobile missile units; 90th Interspecific (Multi-Service) Regional (Training) Centre (MRUTS) of the SMF (Yaroslav Region, Russia) and the Interspecific Regional Training Centre for the SMF (Pskov Region).

Under a directive from the Main Staff of the SMF, the *161st (161-I) Strategic Missile Force Technicians School* (Astrakhan Region) formed in the Yaroslav region as Military Unit 74306 on 1 January 1961. The school was tasked with training personnel in communications operations within the SMF (Yaroslav Region). The 90th Interspecific (Multi-Service) Regional (Training) Centre, Yaroslav Region (lineage going back to the formation of the 10th School of Junior Aviation Specialists on 10 December 1926) was formed as a SMF unit under an order from the Collegium of the Ministry of Defence School in July 1961, being located on an island of Pskov Region. The school was involved in specialist technical training on SMF ICBM complexes. The centre underwent several organisational changes associated with development of the SMF during the Soviet era and following the dissolution of the USSR in December 1991. The organisational name extant in 2020 – Interspecific Regional Centre for the Strategic Missile Forces – came into force in May 1999 – the unit being tasked with training in many tactical areas, including vehicular, complement being established at two training battalions in 2009 (MODRF).

In addition to the above institutions there was the higher military education institution, the Military Academy of the Strategic Missile Forces, named after Peter the Great, which moved to the city of Balashikha in the Moscow region of Russia in 2015. This organisation was tasked with scientific research to formulate and guide the future development of the SMF in regard to the potential for future advanced weapons to ensure a credible nuclear deterrent was maintained by the Russian Federation. The Academy also operated in the interest of other branches of the MODRF (MODRF, 2020).

The Military Academy had its origins in the Officer Department of the Artillery School, which was established in St. Petersburg, Imperial Russia, on 25 November (7 December (Julian)) 1820. The organisations association with rocketry was reinforced in 1943, under the auspices of the Soviet Union, when it commenced training in engineering principles of rocket technology. In 1945, the Soviet Union's primary specialist rocket armament unit was the Department of Armament of the Guards Mortar Units. The Academy was formally incorporated into the SMF of the Soviet Union on 31 December 1959. Following a number of organisational and name changes over several decades, the Academy was formally retitled Military Academy of the Strategic Missile Forces and named after Russian historical figure, Peter the Great, whom had created the first regular army in Russia. In the twenty first century, the primary remit of the Academy was to train officers in engineering for work on modern high technology equipment (Military Academy of the Strategic Missile Forces, 2020).

Organisational and Mobilisation Department of the Strategic Missile Forces (WMD of the SMF) – The Department of the Headquarters of the SMF was established on 31 December 1959. Among the many responsibilities of this organisation was the mobilisation of personnel for and development of the structures of the SMF (MODRF, 2020).

Organisational and Technical Measures on Missile Armament – This organisation was responsible for ensuring the operation of the various missile systems of the SMF, including maintenance and placing same on combat alert. The organisation was responsible for the initial reception of, registering of, storage of, placing in operational use, service life extension and eventual disposal of unspent missiles at the end of their service life (MODRF, 2020).

Page 43-44: Field training with non-operational ICBM transporter launcher vehicles and **PGRK** support vehicles with trainees of the Serpukhov 'branch' of the Military Academy of the Strategic Missile Forces, named after Peter the Great. MODRF

Mobile Regiments of the SMF on patrol route (bottom) and at temporary field position (top). MODRF

Launch of an ICBM from the 480th missile regiment of the 35th missile division of the SMF. MODRF

In 2021, the three missile armies of the SMF and their constituent divisions and the various training, technical and range establishments, continued to operate on a permanent alert status. The number of ICBM's on combat alert would vary as new systems of RS-24 Yars (light) and (then scheduled for 2022) RS-28 Sarmat (heavy) were introduced and older generation systems of the Topol, Topol-M UR-100N UTTX and R-36M2 were replaced.

4

STRATEGIC MISSILE FORCES INTERCONTINENTAL BALLISTIC MISSILE COMPLEXES

In early 2021, the Russian Federation SMF (Strategic Missile Forces) were armed with no less than six types of ICBM (Intercontinental Ballistic Missile) complexes when taking into account the silo and mobile launched variants of Topol-M and Yars. These could be broken down to silo based and mobile based groupings, the former, whilst having no distinct advantage in terms of numbers of deployed ICBM's, accommodated the majority of warheads operated by the SMF. The UR-100N UTTX light silo based ICBM has been progressively retired (replaced by Topol-M and Yars silo based ICBM complexes), with only a few tens of such missiles operationally deployed toward the close of the 2020. From 2019, small numbers of these missiles would be repurposed as the first launch platform for the carriage of Avangard hypersonic glide vehicle warheads designed to defeat the most advanced missile defence systems. The R-36M2 Voevoda heavy ICBM complex had been reduced in numbers from around 48 launch complexes in the mid-2010's to several tens going into 2021. Planning called for this missile complex to be progressively retired from service as constituent missiles reached the end of their operational life and RS-28 Sarmat heavy ICBM's became operational from circa 2022. The mobile missile complexes of RT-2PM Topol and RT-2PM1 Topol-M were progressively being replaced by the RS-24 Yars advanced development of the Topol-M, which featured enhanced capabilities to penetrate advanced missile defence systems. Post-2027 planning called for the silo based missile groupings to consist of RS-24 (silo based) light ICBM and RS-28 Sarmat heavy ICBM complexes. At this juncture the mobile groupings would be predominantly armed with RS-24 Yars ICBM complexes. The RS-26 Rubezh designation covered an advanced derivative of the RS-24, referred to as Yars-S or Yars-M, test launched through the first half of the 2010's.

R-36M2 – The R-36M2 constituted the missile system of the Voevoda strategic strike weapon complex that in turn constituted the heavy ICBM component of the Russian Federation SMF in 2021. The R-36M2 was the last in a long line of OKB-

586 (Yuzhnoye Design Bureau) developed missile complexes carrying the R-36 label over the course of more than five decades of design/development. Development and service, which had commenced with the first generation R-36 family – 8K67 single-warhead ICBM, 8K69 (R-36 Orb) single-warhead FOBS/DICBM (Fractional Orbit Bombardment System/Depressed trajectory Intercontinental Ballistic Missile) and the 8K67P three warhead MRV (Multiple Reentry Vehicle) ICBM (Harkins, 2017).

Test launch of an RS-20B(V) heavy ICBM. KBKHA

The first generation R-36 had been developed by the Soviet Union in response to development of the Titan II silo based ICBM by the United States in the early 1960's, there being no immediately available Soviet equivalent to this super-heavy American missile that was capable of firing a heavy nuclear payload over vast distances. An added impetus, in regard to the 8K69 FOBS, was provided by the inordinate advantage the United States had in deployment of IRBM (Intermediate Range Ballistic Missiles) near to the borders of the USSR (Union of the Soviet Socialist Republics/Soviet Union), something the Soviets, by virtue of geography, were not able to undertake in regard to the contiguous CONUS (Continental United States). This put the Soviet Union at the disadvantage of having to counter large-scale ballistic missile attack from not only the traditional northerly, over the North pole region, direction of CONUS based ICBM's, but also, in regard to attack from Eurasian NATO (North Atlantic Treaty Organisation) territory, westerly and southerly directions. The introduction of the 8K69 provided the Soviet Union with a global reach capability to deliver a large yield nuclear warhead against CONUS targets from multiple directions (Harkins, 2017). The introduction of the RS-28 Sarmat in the post 2021 timeframe would, to a degree, reintroduce a capability for ICBM's to launched against the CONUS and engage the targets from multiple hemispheres, further complicating the work of missile defence systems.

The first 8K67 ICBM launch was conducted on 28 September 1963, almost two months prior to the first launch of a UR-200 (4 November 1963) heavy ICBM (this latter program was not brought to fruition). The first 8K69 FOBS launch was conducted in 1966, followed by the first 8K67P MRV launch in August 1968. Having won out over the UR-200, the R-36 would constitute the heavy element of the Soviet SMF, alongside other ICBM systems, such as the UR-100, which would go on to constitute the primary light ICBM for the SMF – the R-36 and UR-100 were accepted for service on 21 July 1967 (MODRF). Over the next several decades, progressively more capable variants of the R-36 and UR-100 would be introduced to augment and then replace the first generations of these missile complexes.

The first R-36M (START (Strategic Arms Reduction Treaty) index, RS-20A) equipped missile regiment entered combat alert at Dombarovsky, Orenburg, on 25 December 1974. On 18 September 1979, three missile regiments, located at Zhangiztobe, Soviet Kazakhstan, Dombarov, Orenburg and Uzhur in Krasnoyarsk Krai, entered combat alert with the R-36M UTTX(K) (RS-20B) (MODRF). Further capability enhancements would lead to the R-36M2 (RS-20V) Voevoda, which constituted the last Soviet era heavy ICBM complex to attain operational status.

Development of the R-36M2 (designation applied to the overall missile complex with 15A18M technology index applied to the missile) had commenced at Yuzhnoye design bureau, Dnepropetrovsk, Soviet Ukraine (designer Vladimir Fedorovish Utkin), from the R-36M, in August 1983. The missile complex, which carried the NATO reporting index SS-18 Mod 5, 6 and reporting name Satan, was developed as a heavy fourth generation ICBM to provide a viable second strike capability against CONUS targets in an environment of surface blast from nuclear explosions or high altitude nuclear blasts (YDB). This included a requirement for operating in the face of repeated impacts of adversary nuclear warheads on the launch silo district.

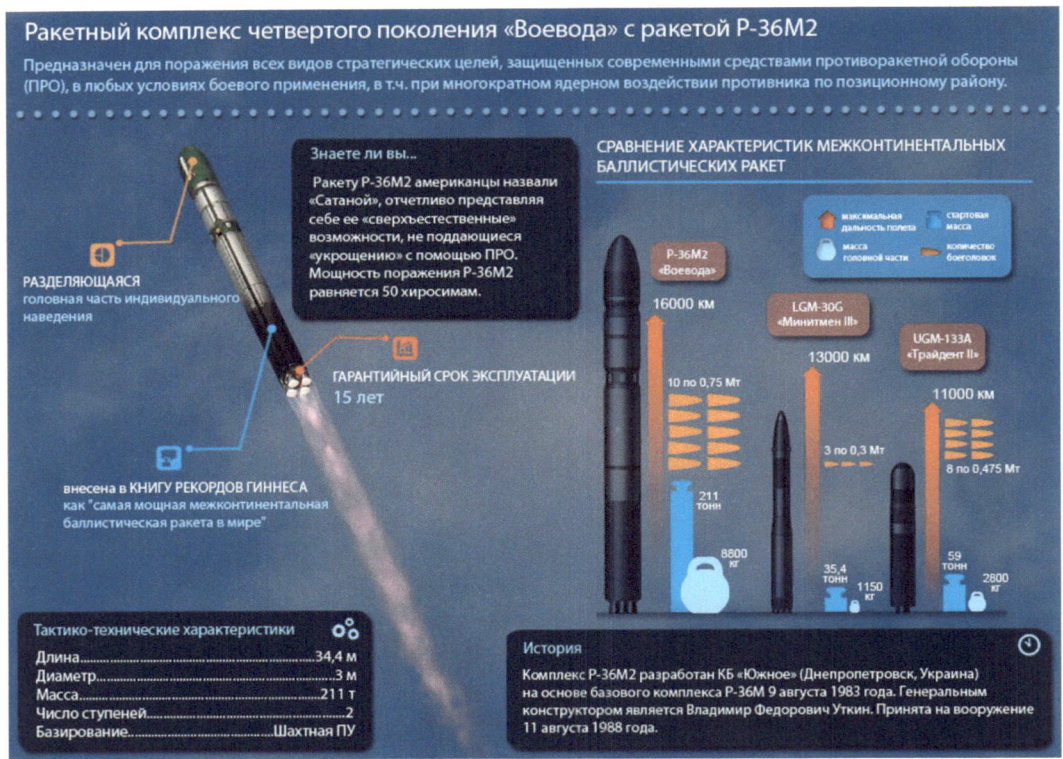

Graphic depicting the R-36M2 Voevoda heavy ICBM complex showing basic characteristics: length, diameter, weight, missile stages etc., brief development dates and comparative data for R-36M2 (range, 18000 km, warheads, 10 x 0.75 Mt and missile/warhead weight, 211 tonne/8800 kg); US ICBM and SLBM – LGM-30G (Minuteman III) (range, 13000 km, warheads, 3 x 0.3 Mt and missile/warhead weight, 35.4 tonne/1150 kg) and UGM-133A (Trident) (range, 11000 km, warheads, 8 x 0.475 Mt and missile/warhead weight, 59 tonne/2800 kg). MODRF

The R-36M2 complex, which adopted the mortar launch system developed for the previous generation R-36M and first successfully tested on 1 November 1976 (YDB History Archive, 1976), incorporated two main stages (a third boost stage was incorporated for ejection of the missile from the launch silo prior to main engine start (mortar launch, noted above)) containerised ICBM armed with a MIRV (Multiple Independently Targetable Reentry Vehicle) warhead section. The engines burned high power output liquid-propellant UDMH fuel with liquid high-boiling hypergolic propellant and NTO oxidizer. Missile length was set at 34.3 m (34.4 m), width, 3 m, launch weight was 211100 kg, or 214300 kg with the MIRV nose section, which could accommodate up to 10 nuclear warheads of 0.55-0.75 Mt (Megaton) yield. The weight of the MIRV head section was put at 2140 kg, although the missile could accommodate a payload of 8800 kg (this was constrained by observing treaty obligations). Maximum firing range was put at 11550 km to 16000 km, dependent upon whether the missile was equipped with a light nose section or a MIRV nose section (MODRF).

Launch of a 15A18M missile of the R-36M ICBM complex. YDB

From its initial deployment the R-36M2 took on the mantle of the world's most powerful ICBM (including intercontinental range SLBM (Submarine Launched Ballistic Missiles), a label it still carried in 2021. Yield from the combined MIRV warheads was, regardless of 0.55 Mt or 0.75 Mt, several hundred times the yield of the atomic bomb dropped on Nagasaki, Japan, in August 1945, and in the order of eight times (assuming 0.75 Mt warheads) the combined yield of the of 3 x 0.3 Mt warheads arming the United States LGM-30G Minuteman III light ICBM complex.

The manufacture to deployment process was eased through complete missile assembly at the build plant and subsequent deployment at the launch complex (silo) with reduced maintenance requirements, improved basing and launch safety and reliability over that attained with previous generation missile systems. The missile control system on the R-36M2 missile complex and ground systems was built around digital computers and a battery of instrumentation to facilitate precise commands between ground control and the missile while on combat alert. The electronic circuits were hardened against the effects of nuclear explosions. The continuous operation of the onboard instrumentation during the period of combat alert and, in the event of missile launch, was facilitated through incorporation of a thermal control system (YDB).

The first regiment of the SMF of the USSR to be armed with the R-36M2 with the MIRV warhead section was placed on combat alert at Dombarovsky, Orenburg,

Region, on 30 July 1988 (MODRF Historical Archive for 30 July 1988) and the missile complex was formally adopted for service with the SMF of the Soviet Union on 11 August that year (MODRF Historical Archive for 11 August 1988).

From initial development through the mid-2010's, thirty three R-36M2 launches were conducted with a success rate of 97.4% (YDB). This equated to only a single launch/flight failure. Having undergone life extension, the R-36M2 underwent force reductions as missiles reached their expiration date. This was accomplished through missiles being launched or retired from service as they reached the end of their fatigue lives. Some 48 R-36M2 complexes were estimated to be active in the SMF in 2017-2018, a small number having been retired since that date, including two withdrawn from service and scrapped in 2020. The several tens of missiles in service in early 2021 are to be replaced by the RS-28 Sarmat heavy ICBM complex from 2022, although it is unclear, in 2021, whether or not this would be on a one for one basis.

R-36M2 Voevoda – data furnished by the MODRF with additional data furnished by Yuzhnoye Design Bureau in parenthesis

Technology Index: 15A18M
Contractual index for START-1: RS-20V
Design department: KB 'Yuzhnoe' [Yuzhnoye Design Bureau], Dnepropetrovsk
General designer: Vladimir Fedorovich Utkin
Missile type: Intercontinental range, two-stage, liquid fueled, MIRV containerised
Basing: Stationary
Start of development: 9 August 1983
In service: 11 August 1988
Maximum range: 11500 km with the light nose section or 16000 km with the MIRV nose section
Number of stages: 2 main stages plus a boost stage
Type of head part: MIRV (with a combined weight of 2140 kg)
Number of warheads: 10
Warhead yield: 0.55-0.75 Mt
Starting weight: 211100 kg (214300 kg with MIRV nose section)
Payload weight: 8800 kg
Length: 34.3 m (34.4 m)
Maximum diameter: 3 m
Propellants: (Liquid, high-boiling hypergolic)
Oxidizer: (NTO)
Fuel: (UDMH)
Warranty period: 15 years

Positioning a 15A18M missile of the R-36M2 ICBM complex, held within its integral launch container, into a silo for placement on combat alert. MODRF

UR-100 – Although the UR-200 and UR-500 programs (the latter formed the basis of the Proton space payload launch vehicle) had not yielded operational ICBM complexes, the experience that resulted from development of the former during the years 1963-1967 would feed into the missile program that the Soviets intended would establish parity with the United States in regard to land based nuclear strike potential (Harkins, 2017). In this respect, the resultant UR-100 series light ICBM would be the Soviet Union's direct counter to the large-scale production and deployment of Minuteman I/II and later Minuteman III ICBM's in the continental United States.

The UR-100 was developed as a light containerised ICBM, constituting the major part of the second generation of Soviet ICBM development/deployment. This system entered mass production and by 1970 around 1,000 were operational with the Strategic Missile Force of the Soviet Union (NPO Mashinostroyenia). By the mid-1980's, four separate series of this complex had been deployed, UR-100к, UR-100U, UR-100N and UR-100N UTTKh (UTTX/UTTH) (RS-18B), the last remaining in small-scale service (several tens) in 2021 (NPO Mashinostroyenia).

Mashinostroyenia was the lead designer on the UR-100 program, which was a collaborative effort involving a number of design bureau, scientific research centres, the Ministry of Defence of the Soviet Union and its subordinates, including the Strategic Missile Force (Mashinostroyenia). The first UR-100 (RS-18) complex went on combat alert at Pervomaisk, Soviet Ukraine, on 26 April 1967. The UR-100 UTTKh (UTTX) was adopted on 1 March 1970 and the UR-100U was adopted for service on 25 September 1973 (MODRF). The UR-100N entered service in 1975, the service life being put at 10 years (NPO Mashinostroyenia). The first regiment equipped with the MR-UR-100 (RS-15A) was placed on combat duty at Bologoe, Tver Oblast, on 8 May 1975. The first missile regiment armed with the MR-UR-100 UTTKh (UTTX) entered combat alert at Bologoe, Tver Oblast on 17 November 1978 (MODRF).

Launch of a UR-100N UTTKh ICBM complex of the Russian Federation Strategic Missile Forces. Mashinostroyenia

Design of the two-stage liquid fueled, containerised silo based UR-100N UTTKh ICBM complex commenced on 16 August 1976, under general designer Vladimir Nikolaevich Chelomey at NGO 'Engineering' (the Design Bureau of Machine Building) Reutov, Moscow region. The ICBM complex, which featured enhanced accuracy over its forebear – UR-100N – carried the START/New START (treaty) index RS-18B, with the missile carrying the technology index 15A35. The UR-100N UTTKh third generation missile complex entered combat alert at Khmelnitsky, Soviet Ukraine, on 6 November 1979, and was formally adopted for service with the Soviet SMF on 17 December that year. The initial 10 year service life of the UR-100N UTTKh was first extended from 10-15 years, then to 25 years, then again to 30 years (Mashinostroyenia), and those in service in 2021 had been extended to 37-38 years. On these values, the assumption has to be that missiles that remained in service from 2018 (in 2018 the UR-100N UTTKh was operational at two SMF sites in the Russian Federation) (Mashinostroyenia)) were from late production, which would be in line with the policy of test launches being conducted with missiles nearest to the end of their projected expiration date, noted below.

Airframe/body of a UR-100N during assembly at NPO Mashinostroyenia. This missile complex would be further developed as the UR-100N UTTKh. Mashinostroyenia

The UR-100N UTTKh engines burned high power output liquid-propellant UDMH fuel with liquid high-boiling hypergolic propellant and NTO oxidizer. Length was set at 24.3 m, diameter, 2.5 m and launch weight was 105600 kg. The missile could accommodate a payload up to 4350 kg. In Russian Federation SMF service the missile complex was armed with six MIRV nuclear warheads in what

NPO Mashinostroyenia described as a 'self-contained unit for warheads dispensing', each warhead capable of generating a yield of 0.55-0.75 Mt. Maximum firing range was put at 10000 km (MODRF).

Page 56: UR-100N UTTKh ICBM complex with outer silo hatch in open position and missile launch container cover still in place. Page 57 top: Head section of 15A35 missile of the UR-100N UTTKh. Page 57 bottom: UR-100N UTTKh silo with outer hatch in open position and missile container cover removed, exposing the 15A35 missile nose section. Mashinostroyenia/MODRF

Launch (distorted) of an RS-18 missile derivative. Mashinostroyenia

The 15A35 missile is housed in an integral launch container, which is itself housed in the missile silo. The container storage incorporated systems for controlling thermal effects and humidity. In the silo the container was placed on a shock absorbing system, which contributed to protecting the missile in the event that the silo complex was subjected to the effects of nuclear explosions prior to missile launch. This contributed to the overall survivability of the complex, allowing it to be deployed even after the silo grouping has been subjected to a nuclear first strike.

The launch of the missile would be conducted remotely and the missile controlled independently and through inertial data input. Deployed UR-100N UTTKh complexes were assessed on the basis of determining the strength of various load-bearing structures and the integrity of the fuel tank walls among many other factors. This determined whether a particular missile required maintenance or needed to be retired. As noted above, the practice of conducting annual test launches of the UR-100N UTTKh was managed on the basis of selecting the missile with the least remaining service life (Mashinostroyenia) – In 2017, the SMF operated in the region of 30 UR-100N UTTKh, the number being reduced by several missiles by 2020.

In line with reducing operational UR-100 complexes to comply with the START-1 arms control treaty, the Russian Federation government had issued a decree on 22 October 1993, authorising a program that would see some UR-100N UTTKh missiles eliminated through usage as launch vehicles for space payloads. This would lead to the introduction of the Strela space payload launch system (Mashinostroyenia).

UR-100N UTTKh – data furnished by MODRF and NPO Mashinostroyenia

Technology Index: 15A35
Contractual index START-1: PC-18B (RS-18B)
Design department: NGO 'Engineering' Reutov
General designer: Vladimir Nikolaevich Chelomey
Missile type: Intercontinental range two-stage, liquid, MIRV containerised
Basing: Stationary (silo)
Start of development: 16 August 1976
In service: 17 December 1980 (MODRF) 17 December 1979 (NPO Mashinostroyenia)
Maximum range: 10000 km
Number of stages: 2
Type of head part: MIRV
Number of warheads: 6
Warhead yield: 0.55-0.75 Mt
Starting weight: 105600 kg
Payload weight: 4350 kg
Length: 24.3 m
Maximum diameter: 2.5 m
Warranty period: 10 years (extended)

A number of UR-100N UTTKh missile complexes, retired from SMF combat alert, would be repurposed as Strela space payload launch vehicles under a Russian Federation government decree dated 22 October 1993. Mashinostroyenia

RT-2PM – As well as introducing new variants of existing systems of the UR-100 series, modernisation of the Soviet and later Russian light ICBM groupings would lead to the introduction of several new systems of the fourth and fifth generations in the late USSR period through the second decade of the twenty first century. Development of new systems of the fourth generation commenced with a research/design program, launched in the mid-1970's, which would ultimately lead to ICBM complexes for silo, rail mobile (RT-23) and road mobile basing over the next several decades. Among these was the RT-2PM Topol (PC-12M (RS-12M) under the START-1 treaty index), with the NATO reporting designation/name SS-25 Sickle. This missile complex, which advanced on the previous generation RT-2P (operational from 1972 until 1994), was developed as a fourth generation mobile ICBM complex, incorporating the missile technology index 15ZH58. The RT-2PM complex was designed/developed by the Moscow Institute of Thermal Technology, under general designers Aleksander Davidovich Nadriadze and Boris Nikolaevish Lagutin, as a three stage (monoblock), solid-fuel complex, silo and mobile based, for service from the mid-1980's (silo based) and late 1980's (mobile based) (MODRF).

Test launch of an ICBM of the Topol-M complex. Academican Pilyugin Centre

The Topol mobile ICBM complex was distinguishable from later Topol-M and Yars complexes by a number of distinctive features, including the large rectangular box type structure on the port forward section of the integral launch silo and the circular antenna complex on the rear port side of the transport launch vehicle. MODRF

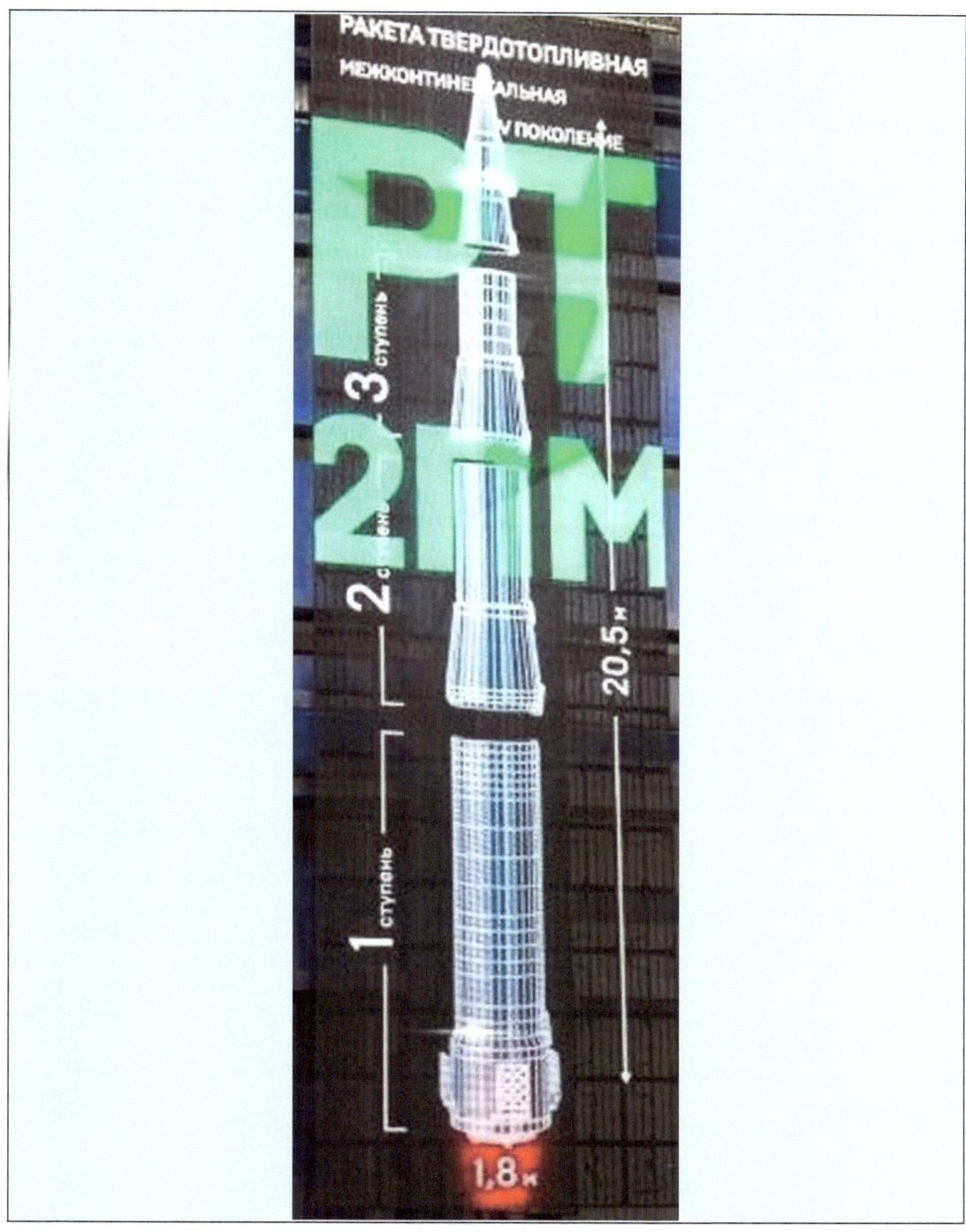

Graphic depicting the various stages – first, second and warhead section – of the RT-2PM Topol ICBM complex, with basic dimensions. MODRF

The Topol complex incorporated a three-stage solid fuel system employing a reactive (mortar) launch start. This ejected the missile from within its integral launch canister, housed in the missile silo (could include fixed silo or mobile silo carried on the 15U168 all-terrain TLV (Transporter Launch Vehicle), prior to first stage engine ignition, which would then propel it on its intercontinental range fight to the target, up to 11000 km distant. The mobile system was carried on and launched from an all-terrain TLV (noted above), incorporating a prominent extendable silo containing the ICBM. The mobile based missile, with a length of 21.5 m and a diameter of 1.8 m, was launched with a start mass of 45.1 tons, of which 1000 kg formed the payload section, accommodating a single nuclear warhead with a yield of 0.55 Mt (MODRF).

Initial design studies for what would become the RT-2PM Topol complex had commenced in 1976, the same year as production of the RSD-10 Pioneer IRBM had commenced at the Votkinsk Zavod plant (Votkinsky Zavod History, 2020). Full-scale development commenced on 19 July 1977, and the first phase of Topol ICBM flight testing commenced in February 1983 (MODRF). That same year, initial preparations were made for a move to serial production, dependent upon a successful flight test program. In the event, the first serial produced Topol complexes were delivered to an operational SMF missile division in 1986 and placed on combat alert that same year. Flight testing continued through December 1987, focused primarily on the mobile based complex, which entered the operational inventory in December 1988 (Votkinsky Zavod History, 2020 & MODRF).

The RT-2PM Topol (NATO reporting designation/name SS-25 Sickle) provided the SMF with a fourth generation ICBM complex that would advance on the capabilities of the previous generation Temp-2S (NATO reporting designation/name SS-16 Sinner). Votkinsky Zavod

Top: RT-2PM Topol mobile missile complex of the Kiev-Zhitomir Order of Kutuzov III (3rd Grade) Missile Division of the Yoshkar-Ola missile formation. Bottom: Test launch of a 15ZH58 ICBM of an RT-2PM Topol complex. MODRF

Topol mobile complexes on patrol routes in various environmental conditions. MODRF

RT-2PM Topol armed mobile missile regiments of the SMF on field deployment (forest environment top) and on local class road surface (bottom). MODRF

Page 68-69: RT-2PM Topol 15U168 TLV and engineering and accommodation vehicles of a SMF mobile missile regiment of the Irkutsk Missile Formation (Vitebsk Guards Red Banner Orders of Lenin) missile division. MODRF

As noted in chapter three, the first Topol missile system was placed on combat alert at Yoshkar-Ola, Mari, in the ASSR (now the Russian Republic of Mari El) on 23 July 1985. On 28 April 1987, the first Topol missile regiment and mobile command post Barrier went on combat alert at Nizhny Tagil, Sverdlovsk region. On 27 May 1988, the first Topol missile regiment equipped with the 'advanced control panel Granit' entered combat alert in Irkutsk and the overall mobile complex was formally adopted for service with the SMF of the Soviet Union on 1 December 1988 (MODRF). The first missile regiment armed with Topol and the new generation 'ASBU' (automated command and control system) entered combat alert at Teikovo, Ivanov region, on 30 December 1988 (MODRF) – in 1999 around 360 Topol complexes were in service in ten SMF missile divisions.

A Topol development, optimised for commercial satellite launch, was delivered in 1996, observing the terms of the START-1 treaty (Votkinsky Zavod History, 2020) – in the period 1993-2006, seven START-1 space payload launch vehicles (the 47000 kg vehicle was capable of delivering a 500 kg payload into low-Earth orbit) from reconfigured RT-2PM ICBM complexes (early launches) were launched from the Plesetsk and Svobodny (now Vostochny) cosmodromes, Russia. In 2020, the chief designer at the Moscow Institute of Thermal Technology confirmed that plans for resuming START-1 launches was being considered to launch small-size satellite clusters.

Topol missile complexes, some retired from SMF alert, were successfully reconfigured and employed as START (START-1) commercial launch vehicles in the period 1993-2006. These commercial launch complexes were painted high visibility yellow in order that they could be distinguished from operational Topol ICBM complexes for verification under the START-1 arms control treaty. *Votkinsky Zavod*

As more modern **PGRK** systems came on strength, older generation complexes of the RT-2PM Topol (bottom) were retired, some being reconfigured as training systems or START-1 commercial launch systems (top), identified by high visibility paint schemes for verification under **START/New START**. CDB Titan

As more advanced ICBM complexes entered the inventory, Topol equipped regiments of the SMF missile divisions embarked upon a drawdown of operational complexes. The silo based complex was superseded by RT-2PM2 Topol-M and RS-24 Yars complexes. By the close of 2017, around 40 Topol PGRK (mobile) complexes remained on alert, this reducing further by 2020, by which time it had been in service as a mobile launched ICBM through the break-up of the Soviet Union in 1991, and almost three decades of service with the SMF of the Russian Federation, and was scheduled to serve into 2024. To keep the complex viable in the face of increased threats posed by missile defence proliferation, the SMF embarked upon a series of force enhancement and life-extension programs. This required the continuance of test launches, some of which would take on an experimental nature. In this regard, an RT-2PM launch was conducted from Kapustin Yar, Astrakhan region, on 5 December 2010 (22.11 hours Moscow time), the inert test warhead impacting the Sary Shagan test range in Kazakhstan. The purpose of this launch, the second RT-2PM launch of 2010 (the other launch had been conducted from the Plesetsk cosmodrome on 28 October that year), was to assess the flight performance of missiles having undergone a service life extension (MODRF, 2010). A Topol ICBM of the Kiev-Zhitomir Orders of Kutuzov Missile Division at the Yoshkar-Ola Missile compound was launched at the Plesetsk cosmodrome at 10.45 am (local) on 3 November 2011 (Yoshkar-Ola Missile Formation (Kiev-Zhitomir Orders of Kutuzov 3rd Grade Missile Division) History, 2020). A test launch of an RT-2PM Topol at the Kapustin Yar facility on 26 September 2017 took on an experimental nature as it was testing advanced technology for enhancing the capability to penetrate the most dense ballistic missile defence systems. The test warhead from the missile accurately impacted the Sary Shagan test range (MODRF, 2017a).

RT-2PM basic information/characteristics – data furnished by the MODRF

Missile Technology Index: 15ZH58
Contractual index, START-1: RS-12M
Design department: Moscow Institute of Thermal Technology
General designer(s): Aleksander Davidovich Nadriadze, Boris Nikolaevish Lagutin
Missile type: Intercontinental range, three-stage (monoblock), solid-fuel
Start system: Active-reactive (mortar)
Basing: Mobile all-terrain transporter launcher vehicle
Start of development: 19 July 1977
Flight test period: February 1983-December 1987
In service: 1 December 1988
Maximum range: 11000 km
Number of warheads/warhead yield: 1 x 0.55 Mt
Starting mass: 45.1 tons
Payload weight: 1000 kg
Length: 21.5 m
Maximum diameter: 1.8 m

RT-2PM test/experimental launches were conducted through the 2010's to determine anti-missile defence systems and life-extension measures effectiveness for service into the 2020's when sufficient RS-24 Yars complexes would be available to effect complete replacement of Topol in mobile missile regiments. MODRF

RT-2PM2 and RT-2PM1 – Topol-M complexes, incorporating the missile technology index 15ZH65 (RT-2MP2) and 15ZH55 (RT-2PM1) and allocated the START-1 index of MS-12M2 (RT-2PM2) and 12M1-RS (RT-2PM1), represented the fifth generation of Soviet and later Russian ICBM design/development. The missile systems, designed as three stage solid-fuel complexes, were developed by the Moscow Institute of Thermal Technology under general designers Boris Lagutin, Semenovich Solomonov and Nikolaevich Yuiry. At the heart of Topol-M capability advances over its forebears was the increased resilience against the effects of nuclear blasts and increased capabilities in regard to systems designed to enable the penetration of a target region protected by missile defence systems.

The missile element of the respective complexes, with a launch mass of 47200 kg, was 21 m in length and had a maximum diameter of 1.86 m. Payload was up to 1200 kg, accommodating a single warhead with a yield of 0.5 Mt. The silo based RT-2PM2 missiles were accommodated in modified complexes formerly occupied by UR-100N UTTKh and R-36M silo based complexes whilst the RT-2PM1 was launched from an integral silo carried on a mobile launch platform. Regardless of mobile or fixed silo basing, missile launch commenced with a reactive mortar ejection from the launch complex canister before the first stage was started to propel the missile on its intercontinental range fight to the target, up to 11550 km distant (MODRF).

Top: The RT-2PM1 and later RS-24 Yars PGRK mobile complexes could be distinguished from the RT-2PM PGRK by a number of distinguishing features, including the more rounded silo nose cone on the latter and the lack of large rectangular box like feature on the port side forward section on the former. Whilst the RT-2PM Topol PGRK transport launch vehicle was centred on the 15U168 all-terrain transporter launch vehicle with integrated missile silo the RT-2PM1 Topol-M and later RS-24 Yars adopted a variation of the MZKT-792210 16x16 TLV with integrated missile silo. MODRF/Press Service of High Precisions Systems Company

Graphics of model representation of the RT-2PM1 Topol M mobile ICBM complex. The model is not intended to be a 100% accurate representation of the Transport Launch Vehicle with integrated extendable missile silo, but does provide a representation of the general layout adopted for the complex and carried over, in modified form, to the RS-24 Yars mobile complex. MODRF

Previous page: 15ZH65 missile test launch from Topol-M complex in winter 2012. This page: The RT-2PM1/2 was a significant technology advance on the RT-2PM and would pave the way for development of the RS-24 Yars. Avangard/CB Titan

Development of Topol-M had commenced in February 1993 and the first twenty tests of the new ICBM complex were successfully completed by 20 December 1994. Successful testing of the first two development missiles was completed in 1996 and RT-2PM2 Topol-M silo based ICBM complexes were delivered to the Strategic Missile Forces in 1998. A 15ZH65 missile was successfully launched on 9 February 2000, bringing the silo based Topol-M flight test phase to a successful conclusion. This paved the way for the silo based Topol-M to be placed on combat alert on 28 April 2000 and formally commissioned into service on 13 July that year. The final launch of the initial flight test phase of the Topol-M mobile ICBM complex was successfully completed on 24 December 2004 and development testing of this complex was successfully concluded toward the end of 2005 ((Votkinsky Zavod History, 2020). This paved the way for the mobile complex to be introduced to operational service in December 2006. In late 2017, around 80 Topol-M complexes remained on combat alert. Topol-M had served as a silo based ICBM complex for more than two decades through 2020 and the mobile variant had served for almost a decade and a half. Both types were being supplanted by more modern missile complexes of the RS-24 Yars, but remained in service with the Strategic Missile Forces in early 2021 (MODRF).

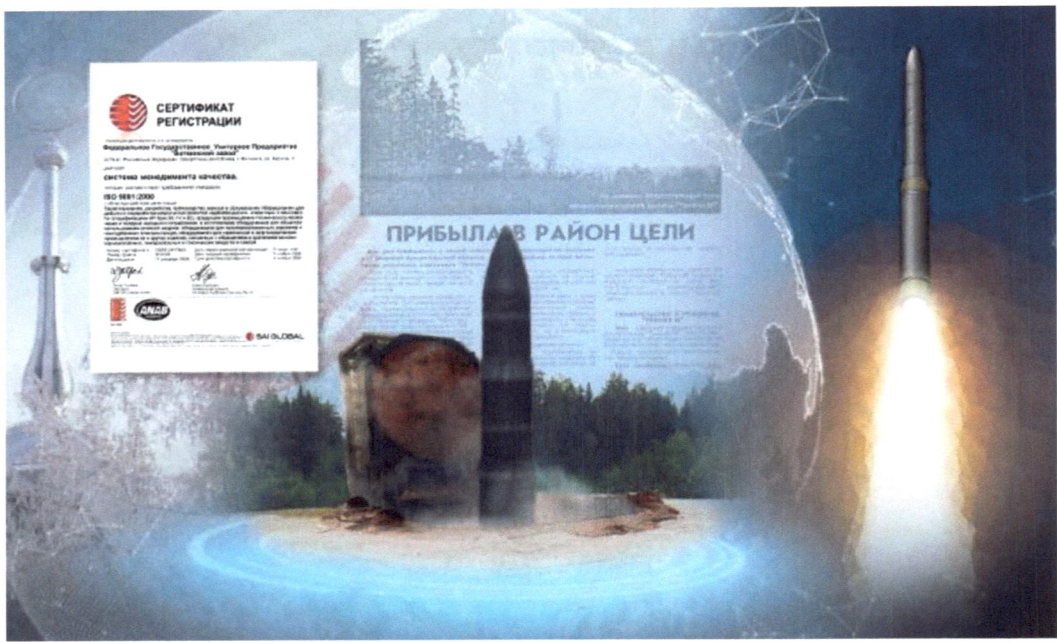

The Topol-M ICBM complex was developed in silo based RT-2PM2 (missile index 15ZH65 and START-1 index MS-12M2 (RS-12M2)) and PGRK (mobile) based RT-2PM1 (missile index 15ZH55 and START-1 index 12M1-RS (RS-12M1)) to supplement and partially replace the RT-2PM Topol fourth generation ICBM complex in Strategic Missile Forces service. Votkinsky Zavod

RT-2PM2/RT-2PM1 ICBM complexes – data furnished by MODRF

Missile technology Index: 15ZH65 (RT-2PM2) and 15ZH55 (RT-2PM1)
Contractual index START-1: MS-12M2 and 12M1-RS
Design department: Moscow Institute of Thermal Technology
General designer(s): Boris Lagutin, Semenovich Solomonov and Nikolaevich Yuiry
Missile type: Intercontinental range three stage, solid-fuel
Basing: Stationary (silo) (RT-2PM2) and mobile (RT-2PM1)
Start of development: February 1993
In service: 28 April 2000 (RT-2PM2) and December 2006 (RT-2PM1)
Maximum firing range: 11550 km
Type of head part: Monoblock (detachable)
Number of warheads: 1
Warhead yield: 0.5 Mt
Starting weight: 47200 kg
Weight of the head portion (warhead vehicle): 1200 kg
Length: 21 m
Maximum diameter: 1.86 m
Warranty period: 15 years

Through the 2010's, the constituent regiments of the mobile missile divisions of the SMF were progressively reequipped with RS-24 Yars PGRK ICBM complexes as older generation RT-2PM complexes reached the end of their service lives. MODRF

Enhanced Fifth Generation/Toward the Sixth Generation ICBM Complexes – In 2002, the US (United States) formally withdrew from the ABM (Anti-Ballistic Missile) treaty (this treaty had limited each party to 100 ABM launchers at one fixed site) that had been entered into with the USSR (inherited by the Russian Federation) in 1972, to prevent any one party from being able to nullify the others nuclear deterrent potential, thereby, keeping the late Cold War MAD (Mutually Assured Destruction) mantra credible. This was deemed necessary to ensure than no one side could conceivably win a nuclear war, thereby reducing the potential that either side would be foolhardy enough to unleash such a conflict. Following the United States withdrawal from the ABM Treaty that nation embarked upon large scale multi-system development and deployment of missile defense systems on land and sea platforms. For the Russian Federation, the testing of Aegis/SM-3 Block IIA missile defence systems against ICBM targets confirmed that NATO claims that such systems were for use against short and intermediate range ballistic missiles only was misinformation designed to stall Russia's work in negating the effectiveness of missile defence systems.

The fifth generation RS-24 Yars ICBM complex was developed to supplement and eventually replace the fourth generation Topol-M ICBM complex. MODRF

It is implausible to expect even the most capable missile defence systems to stop more than a minority of missiles/warheads expected to be launched in a full-scale nuclear exchange. The only realistic scenario for the employment of modern missile defence systems is to be employed in concert with an offensive first strike in which a significant portion of an adversary's nuclear deterrent forces would be destroyed prior to launch, the remaining forces being so sparse that missile defence systems would be able to degrade them to an acceptable number. Of course, for most, this would be the logic of madness. However, from a Russian standpoint, the refusal of NATO to reaffirm the Cold War mantra that no one could win a nuclear war (as noted in chapter 2 the United States acceded, in June 2021, to the Russian request to reaffirm the concept that no one side could win a nuclear war), which, as noted above, had been accepted by both power blocks during the periods of the Cold War era, pointed to increased threat of a nuclear attack on the territory of the Russian Federation. This fear was further reinforced through the dual spectres of the NATO alliance move toward/against and build-up of forces on Russia's borders. This, combined with western withdrawal from arms control and confidence building measures treaties, proliferation of missile defence systems and the introduction of low yield nuclear warheads on SLBM (implemented in 2020) was a genuine cause of concern for the Russian Federation.

To address some of the Russian Federation concerns (some extant at that time and others emerging over the 2000's and 2010's), in the early 2000's that nation, in order to preserve the viability of her nuclear deterrent, embarked upon/enhanced research and development of next generation strategic nuclear payload delivery systems, designed to defeat missile defence systems. This would lead to new generation ICBM's and advanced hypersonic glide vehicle/manoeuvrable warheads optimised to counter missile defence systems.

The first mobile missile regiment assumed combat alert duties with the RS-24 Yars PGRK on 8 August 2011. MODRF

RS-24 Yars – The first of the new Russian ICBM complexes to be introduced in the 2010's was the solid-fuel RS-24 Yars, an advanced development of the Topol-M series ICBM, development of which would have been completed regardless of whether or not the ABM Treaty had survived. Yars was developed through the 2000's by the Moscow Institute of Thermal Technology under General Designer, Academician of the Russian Academy of Sciences, Yuri Solomonov. The concept was formed on the basis of an improved derivative of Topol-M for mobile and silo based operation to supplant Topol and Topol-M complexes. Design of the fifth generation Yars took into account operations of Topol-M to improve the mobile deployment of such systems. Design advancements of the new missile resulted in a heavier complex with a MIRV warhead section (four warheads, each with a yield of between 0.12 to 0.30 Mt) and Yars introduced improvements to the SMF ability to effectively penetrate projected future missile defence systems. Whilst the physical and operational characteristics of Yars remained under a high level of classification in 2021, small releases of information provisioned for calculated estimates of physical characteristics – launch weight; in the region of 50000 kg; length, around 23 m and width, around 2 m.

Yars provided the SMF with a quantum leap in capability, particularly in regard to survivability in the face of the proliferation of missile defence systems. Information from statements of Colonel-General Sergie Karakaev, commander of the SMF, provided for an overview of the capabilities of Yars to overcome missile defence systems from the launch phase through to warhead impact on target up to 11000-12000 km distant. The launch/flight of the Yars missile could be broken down to several phases. The reactive mortar technique, proven on several generations of Soviet and later Russian missile complexes, would eject the missile from the launch container/silo, followed by first stage ignition. This took the missile into the active phase of the flight. Duration of this initial vulnerable phase of flight was set at around three minutes, leaving insufficient time for missile defence system interceptors to be launched and travel the necessary distance to the ICBM launch/active flight region (Aegis Ashore missile defence interceptors have speeds of circa 3.0 km/s (SM-3 Block 1A/B) and 4.5 km/s (SM-3 Block IIA)). The maximum distance travelled in 3 minutes would be 810 km (this would be significantly reduced as less than 3 minutes would be available from interceptor launch and this vehicle would have to travel in the vertical as well as the horizontal planes and conduct correction manoeuvres) whilst Russia's interior covers a distance of in-excess of 5000 km in length and several thousand kilometers from North to South. Added to this was the geographical fact that the vast Russian interior itself largely negated missile defence interceptor capability against ICBM's in the active phase of flight due to insufficient range to cover many potential launch areas. To further complicate the efforts of missile defence systems, the Yars missile could conduct a series of manoeuvres in the active phase of the flight in order to evade missile defence interceptor missiles that operate on hit to kill technology – calculation of impact point on a ballistic collision course. The manoeuvres conducted by Yars effectively transformed it into an aero-ballistic missile invulnerable to interceptor missiles extant in 2021. The initial active phase of flight would be followed by the second stage ignition, third stage ignition then warhead section separation. The warheads, flying at hypersonic speeds up to 7 km/s (25200 km/h), would be deployed in concert with a grouping of decoys simulating active warheads to complicate terminal phase missile defence systems, which, in any-case lacked the speed to conduct successful intercepts – the SM-6 missile system generated a maximum speed of 1.2 km/s (4320 km/h). It remained, in 2021, unclear if the Yars hypersonic warheads could conduct complex manoeuvres in Earth's dense atmospheric layers, but available data suggested that the warheads could manoeuvre to avoid interception by space-based interceptors of advanced missile defence systems.

The PGRK Yars with integrated missile silo had an operational weight of around 100000 kg. The basic chassis, albeit enhanced in characteristics/capability, of the Topol-M, was carried over to Yars, which also adopted a more advanced communications system. Among the advances in capability was that of launch site options. Whereas the Topol generation of PGRK complexes relied on special engineering preparation of launch sites prior to missile deployment, Yars required no-such engineering preparation. Furthermore, Yars was equipped with what was referred to as a flight recalculation system, which enabled the missile to be launched from any point on the PGRK patrol route rather than being constrained within the requirement to deploy to one of a number of pre-designated launch sites, as was the case with the Topol series of PGRK.

Graphic depicting the outer lines of the RS-24 Yars PGRK transport launch vehicle with integrated missile silo for carriage and launch of intercontinental ballistic missile of the Yars complex. This complex featured a number of advances over that of the previous generation Topol, including incorporation of a flight recalculation system, allowing Yars to be launched from any point along a patrol route rather than being restricted to one of a number of predesignated launch sites along the patrol route. MODRF

Page 84-85: RS-24 Yars complex TLV/support vehicle of the Teykovo (Teikov) (Order of Kutuzov Guards Missile Division. MODRF

Missile test launch of an **RS-24 Yars ICBM** complex from the Plesetsk cosmodrome (top) and **RS-24 Yars TLV** with integrated launch silo (bottom). MODRF

Development of Yars continued through the 2000's and service missile complexes were delivered to the SMF in December 2009, individual missile complexes having a planned operational alert period of up to 15 years. The first regiment to be armed with Yars mobile missile complexes entered combat alert with the Teikovo Missile Division, based in central Russia, in March 2011. By November 2019, around 150 Yars complexes (mobile and silo based) had been delivered to the SMF. By late 2020, six mobile missile divisions had been rearmed with Yars mobile complexes. The SMF intended to complete its Yars (silo and mobile) rearmament program in 2024 (Chief Designer, MITT, 2020).

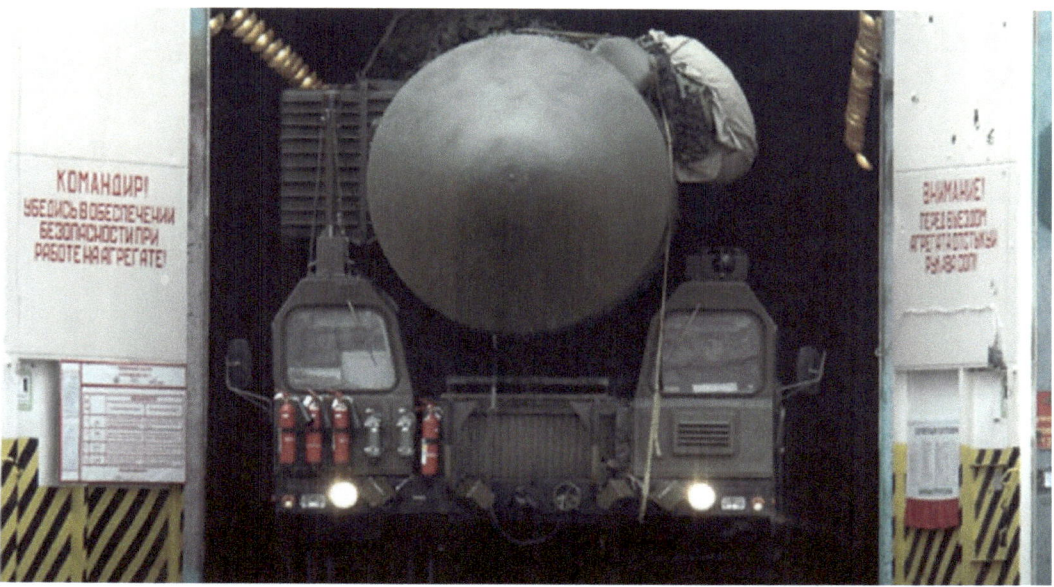

Top: PGRK ICBM complex in the Sverdlovsk region in October 2020. Bottom: PGRK convoy during the first summer period training exercise in the Irkutsk region in early June 2021. MODRF

Top: **PGRK RS-24 Yars** road training complex, circa 11 June 2021, utilised to prepare crews for allocation to alert status. Bottom: SMF autonomous launcher driver/mechanic training unit. MODRF

Top: RS-24 Yars PGRK transport launch vehicle with integrated launch silo. Bottom: RS-24 PGRK Yars complex of the Yoshkar-Ola missile formation manoeuvres on unpaved patrol route surface circa 13 August 2021. CDB Titan/MODRF

Ground security for SMF mobile missile division whilst on deterrence patrol was provided by mobile anti-sabotage troops, which were equipped with several types of armoured support vehicles. MODRF

The Topol, Topol-M and Yars PGRK (mobile) ICBM complexes incorporated a wide diversity of vehicles that supported the functions of defence, engineering and staffing. Some of the vehicular systems had been in service for a considerable time as part of a number of PGRK missile systems, including TEMP-2S, RSD-10 Pioneer, Pioneer K and Pioneer UTTKh. There were, of course, other vehicles, such as the UTM-80M decontamination vehicle, Typhoon-M armoured personnel carrier/combat vehicle (Harkins, 2020). Miscellaneous vehicle systems of the mobile missile divisions could include: 15V75 communication vehicle; 15V148 specialised system support vehicle; 15V167 combat control vehicle; 15V179 communications vehicle; 15M107 remote mine disarming vehicle; 15G218 STAD-100 transportable nitrogen/oxygen producing station; 15T117 mess vehicle; 15T118 accommodation vehicle; 15M69 engineering support and camouflage vehicle; 15U168 TLV vehicle for Topol missile, MZKT-792210 16x16 TLV for the Topol-M (carried over to Yars) and the 3F-30-9 conveyor loading unit (MODRF). The PGRK divisions were also supported by specialist UAV (Uninhabited Air Vehicle) units and detachments operating the Peresvet combat laser system to protect the mobile formations from airborne (potentially space-borne) threats whilst on the move or when stationary at a deployment site (Harkins, 2019).

MZKT-792210 16x16 Technical Characteristics – data furnished by Volat, Minsk Wheel Tractor Plant, Republic of Belarus

Gross vehicle weight: 124000 kg
Curb vehicle weight: 44000 kg
Payload: 80000 kg
Engine & Transmission
Type: YAMZ-847.1 diesel, V-shape, 12-cylinder
Power: 588 kW (800 hp.) at 2100 min^{-1}
Maximum torque: 3090 Nm at 1400-1500 revolutions per minute
Transmission type: MZKT hydromechanics
Driving axles: Central reduction gears with inter-axle and cross-axle, planetary wheel hub reduction
Axle suspension: Inter-dependent hydro-pneumatical, steering system, braking system, tyres and frame
Steering system: Left/right hand drive, hydraulic power assisted
Brake system: Duel-circuit with pneumo-hydraulic drive
Tyres: 1600x600-685, central tyre inflation system, off-road protector
Frame: Rigid frame, longitudinal, equipped in front with two towing forks and rear towing hook
CAB: 2, left – 2-seats, right – 1-seat. Equipped with controls and instrumentation
Nominal voltage: 24V
Batteries: 4 x 380Ah

Top: Missile regiment of the Yoshkar-Ola missile Formation re-equipped with **RS-24 Yars PGRK** in the late 2010's. Bottom: **RS-24 Yars PGRK** field deployment in winter conditions. MODRF

Top: Missile test launch of an RS-24 Yars complex. Bottom: The MZKT-792210 based TLV of an RS-24 Yars PGRK is ferried across a water obstacle by a Russian armed forces PP-2205M pontoon complex on 25 May 2019. MODRF

Top: RS-24 Yars PGRK complex. Bottom: Yars PGRK complex of the Barnaul or Tagil missile formations on a patrol route circa summer 2021. CDB Titan/MODRF

A quartet of **RS-24 PGRK** complexes arriving in the Moscow region for participation in the 2020 Victory Parade. MODRF

PGRK RS-24 Yars complex being ferried across the Oka River, Russia, circa 28 July 2021. MODRF

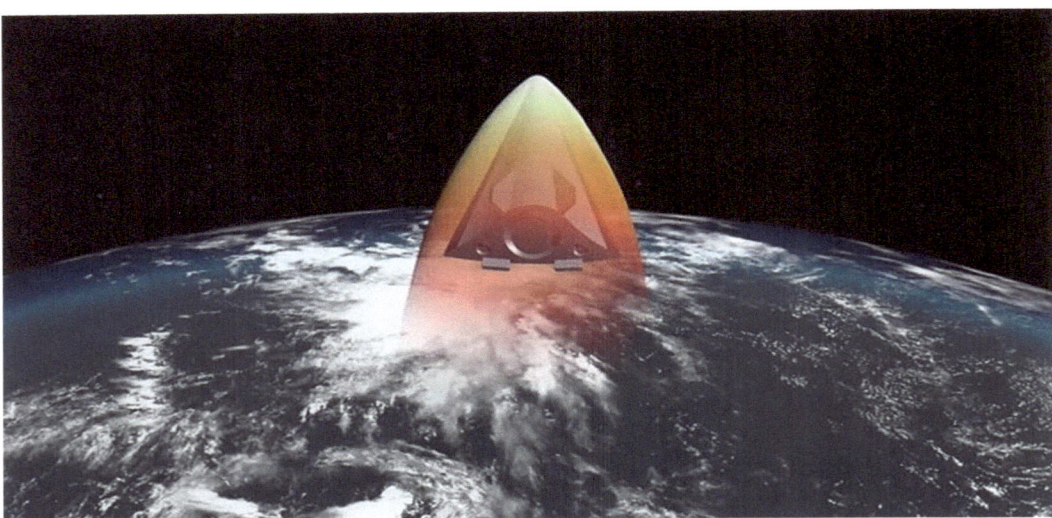

The Sarmat and Avangard strategic strike complexes have been developed to counter the proliferation of NATO missile defence systems. MODRF

Avangard and Sarmat – The RS-28 Sarmat heavy ICBM complex, developed as a replacement for the R-36M2 Voevoda, and the Avangard hypersonic glide vehicle, were developed to ensure the viability of the Russian strategic nuclear deterrent in the face of NATO missile defence systems proliferation. The RS-28 Sarmat missile was designed with a reduced boost phase to mitigate vulnerability in the ascent and incorporated a MIRV section armed with high speed maneuverable warheads. It was expected that the Sarmat vehicle could be armed with the Avangard hypersonic glide vehicle, although this had not been confirmed in 2021. The designer/developer of Sarmat, GRT State Missile Centre Makeyev, had developed a high speed (expected to be hypersonic and potentially high supersonic in the terminal phase) for employment by sea based SLBM (RS-30 Bulava) (chief designers, Yuri Solomonov & Alexander Sukhodolosky) and land based ICBM (considered to be Sarmat).

The road to advanced maneuverable warheads of the Makeyev and Avangard types can be traced back to the 1960's, when two separate sub-orbital/atmospheric maneuvering warheads were developed for the UR-200/UR-500 sub-orbital weapon programs. The AB-200 warhead had been developed to arm the IBM UR-200 ICBM and the AB-500 warhead was developed to arm the larger IBM UR-500 ICBM. These warheads were designed in such a manner as to be capable of maneuvering in Earth's atmosphere after de-orbit to increase accuracy. To this end, OKB-52 developed the MP-1 vehicle, which was to be capable of employing aerodynamic control to maneuver in Earth atmosphere at high hypersonic speeds, this having been accomplished in what was described as a successful test in 1961, when the UR-200 was under development (this program was later cancelled) (Harkins, 2017).

The early successes of these programs did not lead to the short or medium term introduction of ICBM warheads capable of maneuvering in the dense layers of Earth's atmosphere. However, despite the harsh economic climate of the decade or so following the break-up of the Soviet Union in 1991, it appears that the Russian Federation retained a technology base in this area. This placed her in a forthright position to develop manoeuvrable exo-atmospheric and atmospheric warheads in response to the United States withdrawal from the ABM Treaty in 2002 and the subsequent development and introduction of advanced missile defence systems with the potential to erode the Russian nuclear deterrent force of Soviet era legacy systems. This would lead to the Avangard hypersonic glide vehicle and maneuverable warheads capable of evading missile defence systems, which, in regard to their potential against the new Russian strategic missile systems, had been rendered obsolete.

RS-28 Sarmat heavy ICBM complex. GRT Makeyev

Top: **RS-28 Sarmat** test missile/launch canister being installed in a launch silo during the development phase. Above: A Sarmat representative calibrated test airframe is propelled from a launch silo during pop up tests of the reactive mortar launch system, whereby the missile is ejected from the silo prior to first stage engine ignition. MODRF

As noted above, the Sarmat heavy ICBM complex was developed as a direct replacement for the R-36M2 heavy ICBM complex. In this regard, Sarmat would take on from the R-36M2 the mantle of the largest most powerful ICBM in the world, whilst significantly improving on previous generation missile technology capabilities in a number of realms, including the ability to successfully penetrate missile defense systems to strike key strategic targets of any state attacking the Russian Federation with nuclear weapons.

The principle of operation for Sarmat was the delivery of warheads on flight trajectories designed to defeat missile defence systems. In 2020, the complex had a reported range in the region of 18000 km, facilitating for the delivery of warheads from multi-hemispheric directions, presenting particular problems for potential future missile defence systems. Launch weight was in the region of 208.1 tons and payload was in the region of 10 tons – as of mid-2021 there had been no official release in regard to numbers and yield of the MIRV warheads, but at 10 tons payload this would be expected to be in the region of six to ten, each with yields in the 0.5-0.75 Mt range, depending on type.

In December 2019, the Russian Defence Ministry confirmed that Sarmat would be armed with advanced hypersonic warheads, but could also, if required, carry existing warheads employed by legacy missile complexes (MODRF). Whilst this confirmed that maneuverable warheads would be employed on the missile, it remained a point of contention whether this referred to the maneuverable warhead developed by GRT Makeyev. This unit was described by Makeyev as a high velocity maneuverable warhead for ground based and sea-based missiles, suggesting that it may have formed the warhead element of the RS-30 Bulava as well as Sarmat.

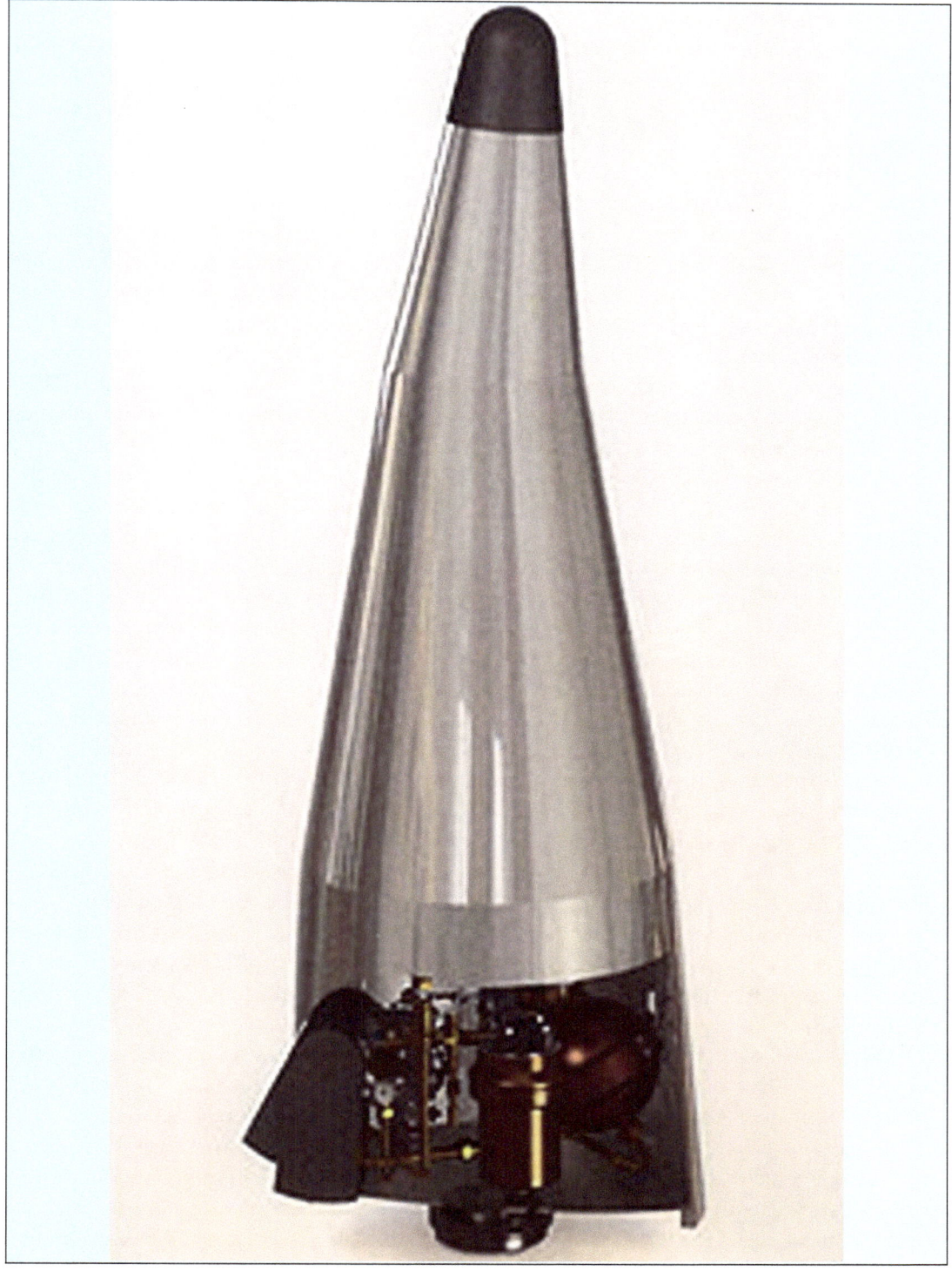

Page 102: Sarmat missile launch container being transported from the manufacturer to a test facility, circa 2018-2020. **This page:** High velocity maneuverable warhead designed for Russian strategic missile systems in the 2020's. MODRF/GRT Makeyev

The MODRF had issued a research and development contract in June 2011 (MDB Release on Sarmat R&D). This was under the auspices of a decree of the Russian Federation government defence order and forward planning for the period covering 2012-2013, which was the catalyst for full-scale research and development of the Sarmat ICBM complex by MDB (Makeyev Design Bureau). General designer on the Sarmat program was V.G. Degtiar with Yu. A. Kaverin as Chief Designer.

By 2018, MDB confirmed that much of the ground testing, including the propulsion system, of the Sarmat system had been successfully completed, paving the way for further testing, assembly of test missiles and ground infrastructure for launch. This latter area involved significant infrastructure work to be conducted at the Plesetsk cosmodrome, North Russia, from where test launches were initially expected be conducted. It was confirmed in December 2018 that the rearmament schedule for the heavy ICBM formations called for introduction of the Sarmat ICBM in 2021. The first examples would be put on combat alert with the Uzhursk missile formation, which was armed with the R-36M2 missile system in 2018 (Detail from Commander of the SMF, Colonel-General Sergey Karakaev, 2018), remaining so in 2021. In a release dated 3 February 2020, the Deputy Defence Minister of the Russian Federation stated that flight testing of the RS-28 Sarmat would be completed in 2021, serial deliveries would commence that year and the first missiles would be placed on combat alert before the year was out (Deputy Defence Minister of the Russian Federation, 3 February 2020), reinforcing statements made to this effect in 2018. In early May 2021, news releases, citing unnamed sources within the Russian defence industry (unnamed sources should be treated with caution), suggested that Russia intended to test flight three Sarmat ICBM's, one at the maximum range out to 18000 km, from the third quarter of 2021 (TASS, 2021). The month prior, it had been confirmed that planning now called for attainment of combat alert in late 2022 (refer to chapter 6). The Russian Deputy Defence Minister had, on 30 December 2020, confirmed that Sarmat reactive mortar (pop-up) trials – for propelling the missile out of the launch silo prior to main engine ignition – had been completed (MODRF). Sarmat flight testing had been expected to be conducted from the Plesetsk Cosmodrome (noted above). In December 2020, it was confirmed that Sarmat testing was then scheduled to be conducted at the Severo-Yeniseysky proving ground, Krasnoyarsk Krai, Siberia, from the second half of 2021 (Expanded Meeting of the Defence Ministry Board, 2020).

Avangard – The Avangard hypersonic glide vehicle that entered combat alert with the SMF in December 2019 was not an ICBM weapon complex, but rather a revolutionary new warhead system that could be installed on new generation and existing ICBM complexes, such as the UR-100N UTTX light silo based ICBM – the first carrier vehicle application for Avangard. The Avangard system was designed to penetrate any existing and hypothesised future anti-missile defence shield through a series of measures. The glide vehicle itself was designed to maneuver in the upper and lower (dense regions) of the atmosphere at speeds in excess of Mach 20 (twenty times the speed of sound), provisioning a system that would be invulnerable to missile defence interceptor systems.

While there had been a number of assertions, the actual main developer of the Avangard system had not been formally disclosed as of mid-2021. The most reliable information then at hand suggested that the system was developed by the Research and Production Association of Machine Building located in Reutov in the Moscow Region of Russia. Again, with no official confirmation, leaked data suggested that the system commenced initial flight testing in 2004, some two years after the demise of the ABM Treaty. However, the concept dated back some considerable time prior to that. The initial program that led to Avangard had emerged as a direct response to the United States SDI (Space Defence Initiative) activities – the United States anti-ballistic missile defence program (that emerged in the early 1980's (later cancelled) under the authorisation of the Reagan administration.

When SDI, widely referred to as the 'Star Wars' program, was made public, the Soviet leadership responded by passing a resolution authorising development of various measures to counter the American program, which would, in effect, have nullified the vastly expensive and overly ambitious attempt by the United States to neutralise the potential of the Soviet nuclear deterrent. From a Soviet standpoint, this was viewed as the western block creating the potential for a nuclear first strike against the USSR to destroy most of her nuclear deterrent forces on the ground, with SDI technology being employed to intercept a significant number of the vastly reduced Soviet strategic nuclear strike assets that would be expected to respond. Among the measures undertaken had been improvement of existing ICBM complexes leading to the R-36M2, designed to operate after a nuclear first strike on its base location. Other more radical solutions to neutralising the threat posed by SDI was the initiation of development programs to arrive at weapon systems able to evade missile defence systems hypothesised for the SDI program. Among these solutions was the concept of the hypersonic glide vehicle armed with nuclear warhead(s) to arm Soviet ICBM's, work on which had commenced in 1985. This was confirmed by PDEMB, Hon. CEO, Chief Designer, Gerbert Yefremov, in an interview conducted in 2020.

The development of hypersonic glide vehicles continued through the break-up of the Soviet Union in 1991 and through the first decade of the twenty first century. This included extensive ground testing, including laboratory bench tests, and a program of flight tests employing UR-100N UTTKh light ICBM's – such flight tests continued in the first years of the 2000's. The MODRF confirmed that the combat maneuverable unit carrying the Avangard hypersonic glide vehicle was taken from the UR-100N UTTKh and that this would be adapted to be incorporated into other ICBM systems under development (Expanded Meeting of the Defence Ministry Board, 2020).

The announcement of the US intention to withdraw from the ABM Treaty placed the Russian Federation in a similar position to that faced by the Soviet Union in the mid-1980's – the United States attempting to neutralise her (Russian) nuclear deterrent potential with all the consequences that this entailed. Work on hypersonic glide vehicles was reinvigorated under the direct authorisation of the President of the Russian Federation. To this end, work on a practical hypersonic glide vehicle, intended for potential deployment as a weapon system, commenced in 2004 (noted above) and continued through the final test launch conducted in December 2018. On the 17th of that month, the commander of the SMF confirmed that a batch of Avangard had entered serial production for allocation to and placement on combat alert with the Dombarovsky (1st) Missile Regiment before the end of 2019 (Detail from Commander of the SMF, Colonel-General Sergey Karakaev, 2018). In the event, Avangard armed missiles assumed combat alert with the 1st Missile Regiment of the SMF at Orenburg, Urals, in late December 2019 (MODRF Board, 2020).

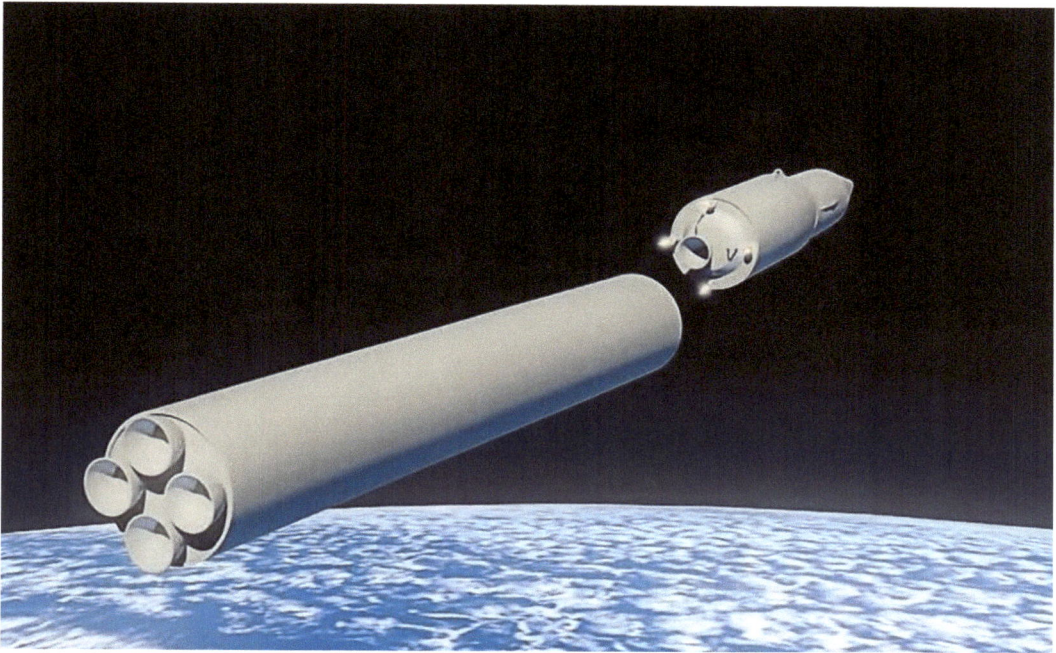

Page 106-107 top: Trio of images showing the installation of an Avangard hypersonic glide vehicle on what is thought to be a **UR-100N UTTX ICBM** complex at the launch silo. Note the open silo hatch in the background. Page 107 bottom: Graphic depicting the ICBM warhead stage, carrying the Avangard hypersonic glide vehicle, separating from the missile body stage. MODRF

The limited capability with the two Avangard systems placed on combat alert in the Urals in December 2019 was extended/enhanced in 2020, this being confirmed in October that year when the Russian Defence Minister, Sergie Shoigu, reported that the necessary work for activation of two more Avangard systems would be completed at the Orenburg missile complex before the end of 2020. As part of its efforts to persuade the United States to extend the New START treaty, Russia provided an opportunity for American arms control officials to inspect the Avangard missile system, incorporating the hypersonic glide vehicle, over 24-26 November 2020 (MODRF). This was to no avail, but the treaty was eventually salvaged in February 2021 (noted above), when the new incoming administration in the United States agreed to the five year extension that Russia had been urging.

Graphic depicting the warhead stage discarding its protective covers to reveal the Avangard hypersonic glide vehicle in advance of its release on a sub-orbital flight before reentering the atmosphere to manoeuvre to the designated target. This graphic would suggest that, for test purposes at least, the UR-100N UTTX carrier vehicle was configured for only a single Avangard warhead. MODRF

The introduction of Yars, Avangard and later Sarmat, together with other non-SMF systems, such as the Kinzhal 1000+ km range class air launched hypersonic missile, Tsirkon (Zircon) 1000+ km range class surface and submarine launched hypersonic missile, Iskander-M short-range (500 km class) aero-ballistic missile, and the Poseidon Multi-Purpose Oceanic System, have created an environment that has nullified two decades of United States/NATO missile defence development and deployment. Avangard, Sarmat and Yars ensuring the viability of the SMF capability to launch a counter strike in the event of an attack on the Russian Federation with nuclear weapons launched by any aggressor state.

5

MISSILE ATTACK WARNING SYSTEM OF THE MISSILE DEFENCE FORCES

The Soviet command and control network for ICBM (Intercontinental Ballistic Missile) and spacecraft in Earth orbit had its early beginnings following the 1955 decision to build the ICBM test facility (now part of what is known as Baikonur Cosmodrome) in Soviet Kazakhstan (now an independent republic). This KIK (Ground Control Station) attained operational capability in 1957, the year of the first successful ICBM launch and the first artificial satellite to be placed in Earth orbit. Construction commenced for an ICBM test range in the Arkhangelsk district (the present day Plesetsk Cosmodrome) in 1957, and, in 1960, the 3rd Department of the Main Missile Directorate of the Ministry of Defense of the USSR (Union of Soviet Socialist Republics – Soviet Union) was formed to facilitate the organisation of space control. This was formed into the Central Spacecraft Directorate of the USSR Defense Ministry in 1964 (MODRF).

By the late 1950's, the USSR air defence network, for the detection and engagement of airborne threats to the Soviet Union and Warsaw Pact nations, was well advanced and progress was being made in the realms of closing down high altitude operations by United States Lockheed U-2 strategic reconnaissance aircraft. It was identified that detection of long-range ballistic missiles would become a priority as these weapons were expected to overtake the manned strategic bomber as the main threat capable of delivering nuclear warheads against Soviet strategic targets over the coming decade. Whilst development of infrastructure was ongoing for the control of ICBM launches and spacecraft operations, it was necessary to develop a widespread chain of systems for the timely detection of an attack on the territory of the USSR and Warsaw Pact nations by ballistic missiles, expected to be armed with nuclear warheads. This led to several generations of space based and land based surveillance systems to ensure detection of a ballistic missile attack against the Soviet Union and later the Russian Federation in order that a timely response could be implemented through a counterstrike, ensuring the doctrine of MAD (Mutually Assured Destruction).

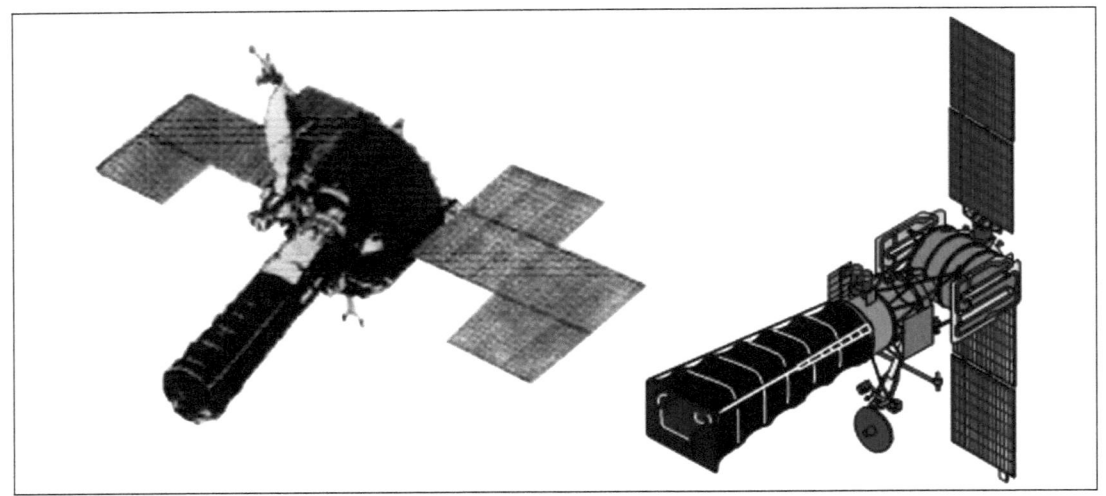

The first line of defence in the Russian Federation missile attack warning system was a constellation of satellites equipped with a suite of advanced infrared monitoring sensors able to detect missile launches against any environmental background. The onboard sensors would track the missile flight from launch, through the boost phase and into sub-orbit in order to determine the potential target and calculate warhead impact area. MODRF

Missile Attack Warning – In 2021, the Russian Federation system of early warning of ballistic missile attack consisted of a two-tier defence line. The first of these was the space based satellite cluster able to detect the launches of ballistic missiles on land or ocean surfaces of the planet. The second tier of defence was centred on a line of Veronezh-DM/M ballistic missile warning radars, providing a duel metre-decimetre wave range radio-electronic coverage on the periphery of the territory of the Russian Federation. In circa 2016, prefabricated Veronezh-DM systems were put on combat alert in Yeniseysk and Barnaul and a Veronezh-M system was to be put on combat alert in Orsk (MODRF Board, 2015). In addition there were other systems that were directly integrated into the missile attack warning system, including the Volga radar complex, the Okno (Window) Optical-electronic complex, Krono complex and the Don-2N multifunctional radar station.

The primary missile attack warning system was based around a cluster of Tundra satellites of the Kupol Unified Space System – a third generation space based warning complex developed to replace the Oka and Oka-1 satellite cluster developed in the Soviet era. The satellites, placed in elliptical orbits, incorporated a suite of advanced infrared monitoring sensors able to detect missile launches against any environmental background, noted above. The onboard sensors tracked the missile(s) flight from launch, through the boost phase and into orbit in order to determine the potential target and calculate warhead impact area(s). The addition of the fourth Tundra satellite facilitated the Kupol Unified Space System (expected to grow to a nine satellite cluster) to attain a minimum operational capability in summer 2020.

In 2021, Veronezh-DM/M radar complexes constituted the major element of the ground based tier of the Russian Missile Attack Warning System. MODRF

The second tier of the missile attack warning system was centred on the ground based Veronezh-DM/M radar complexes. These systems, developed by OJSC Radio Engineering Institute, A.L. Mints, Moscow, provided for timely detection of ballistic missiles on flight profiles taking them into radar coverage. The radar tracked the missile(s) and calculated coordinates of the their intended target(s) through calculation of various parameters of the detected missile(s), such as motion, and automatically provided data on the missile(s)/warhead(s) target and the status of potential interference (jamming). The radar system, operating in the decimeter wave range, had a power consumption of 0.7 MW and could detect targets out to a range of 4200 km (MODRF, 2020).

Under the plan to create a modern two-wave ground based missile attack warning radar coverage, the chief designer at the Research Institute for Long-Range Communications (part of RTI Group) confirmed that the MODRF had installed an improved Veronezh radar complex, referred to as Yakhorama, in Crimea, Southern Military District. This reinforced a statement from the Russian Defence Minister in December 2020 that work on construction of a Yakhoroma station in Sevastopol, Crimea, would commence in 2021. The metre wavelength Yakhoroma complex would be positioned between the two decimeter wavelength radar stations in Armavir, several hundred km North Easterly from Novorossiysk on the Russian Black Sea coast and Kaliningrad on the Baltic Sea Coast. Extant metre wavelength radar stations in service in early 2021 were expected to be modernised, incorporating technology advances developed for systems, such as Yakhorama. Longer term, Russia intended to replace all previous generation missile attack warning radar systems with Veronezh/Yakhorama stations – this latter system, a further unit of which was scheduled to be placed on alert in the region of the Chukchi Sea by 2030 (in uninhabited autonomous operation mode), operated in four frequency wave ranges: centimeter, metre, decimeter and millimetre. This was confirmed in mid-

February 2021 by Andrei Revonok, chief of the Russian Space Troops Main Centre for the Missile Attack Warning section of the Aerospace Force (MODRF).

Daryal radar complex of the Russian Federation missile attack warning system entered alert in 1983. The system enhanced the Soviet Union and later Russian Federation ability to detect ballistic missiles on flight profiles taking them into radar coverage, as well as space objects in low Earth orbit and sub-orbital targets. MODRF

The Veronezh radar complexes initially supplemented, and were intended to replace, previous generation systems of the Daryal, Volga and Dnepr (Dnestr) types. The Daryal, developed by OJSC A.L. Mints, Moscow, and commissioned in 1983, provided for detection of ballistic missiles on flight profiles taking them into radar coverage, as well as space objects in low Earth orbit and sub-orbital targets. The radar complex tracked the missile(s) and calculated the coordinates of the their intended target(s) through calculation of various parameters of the detected missile(s), such as motion, and automatically provided data on missile/warhead launch area, calculated target area and the status of potential interference (jamming). This large radar system consisted of four main components: a command and measurement centre; transmitting radio engineering centre; repair and calibration base; communication centre and information transfer. The radar, operating in the meter wave range, could detect targets out to a distance of 6000 km at up to 90° in azimuth and up to 40° in elevation.

The Volga radar complex, developed by AO NPK NIIDAR, Moscow, and commissioned into service in 2003, provided for automatic detection of ballistic missiles on flight profiles taking them into radar coverage, as well as space objects in low Earth orbit and sub-orbital targets. The radar complex tracked the missile(s) and calculated the coordinates of their intended target(s) through analysis of various parameters of the detected missile(s), such as motion, and automatically provided data on the missile/warhead launch area, calculated target area and the status of potential interference (jamming). These large radar systems consisted of three main components: the data transmission system; computing system and the command post. The radar system, operating in the decimeter wave range, could detect targets out to a range of 2000 km.

All of the ground based missile defence radar complexes were designed to operate in continuous duty mode in compliance with their constant combat alert status.

The Volga radar complex of the Russian Federation missile attack warning system. MODRF

Under Russian commitments to bring all terrestrial assets of the SMF (Strategic Missile Forces) and the missile attack warning system within the state borders of the Russian Federation, the agreement on the Russian usage of the Balkhash radar station, located on the territory of Kazakhstan, was terminated under a decree passed by the Russian State Duma (Russia's Lower House of Parliament) on 21 July 2020. The Balkhash radar station had been the key element of the ground based missile attack warning in the Russian missile attack warning system covering the southern direction prior to being withdrawn from combat alert on 1 June 2020. The radar system had been rendered redundant due to the introduction of the four advanced Veronezh series radars within the territory of the Russian Federation, noted above. Under its commitment to provide data on missile attack warning to the Republic of Kazakhstan, Russia developed the Krokus warning system, which was to be completed in Kazakhstan during 2020 (Russian Space Force Commander (Alexander Golovko) statement, 22 July 2020).

The Okno (Window) optical-electronic complex surveyed the near-Earth space environment and reported on objects determined to be of artificial origin. MODRF

Other elements of the missile attack warning system included the Okno Optical-electronic complex, tasked with surveying the near-Earth space environment and reporting on objects determined to be of artificial (non-natural) origin, which were than classified and their intended function determined, including their state of motion. The system, developed by OJSC Krasnogorsk plant, S.A. Zverev, and placed on combat alert in 1999, consisted of three main components: The optoelectronic search stations; search station detection complex and the communications/information transfer station. The system operated in visible spectrums in ranges of 0-360° in azimuth and 30-90° in elevation and could detect space objects at altitudes up 50000 km, considerably in excess of geostationary orbit. The optoelectronic station, employed for photometry and the measurement of detected object angular coordinates, operated in the visible spectrum in 360° azimuth and 20-90° in elevation. To conduct the assigned tasking's, the system was equipped with 500 mm diameter narrow-angle channel lenses, 235 mm diameter wide-angle channel lenses and tracked targets with an angular speed of 3.7°/second (MODRF).

The Don-2N multifunctional radar station entered combat alert in 1991. MODRF

The Don-2N multifunctional radar station (construction commenced in 1978 and the system entered combat alert in 1991) was an element of the missile defence systems covering Moscow and the central industrial region. The radar was incorporated into the wider missile attack warning systems located on the periphery of the territory of the Russian Federation. The Don-2N, which operated in the meter wave range, could detect objects as small as 5 cm at altitude ranges of 600-1000 km (covering all standard ICBM flight profiles) in an angular range of 360° in azimuth with coordinate measurement accuracy of 200 m in range and 0.02-0.04° in elevation (MODRF, 2020). The system was updated for service in the 2020's, enabling it to better detect smaller/low observable warheads.

The Krono Radio-optical complex for identification of space objects. MODRF

Another element of the space control system, which, in practice, contributed to the missile attack warning system, was the Krono complex, which could autonomously detect space objects in low-Earth orbit and determine their parameters of trajectory.

The various elements of the missile attack warning system bestowed a highly efficient means for providing the Russian Federation political/military higher command with timely data on a potential missile attack in order that objective decisions could be made on threat assessment and, if required, ensure a retaliatory response from the Russian Strategic Nuclear Forces, incorporating the Strategic Missile Forces, cruise missile armed aircraft of Long Range Aviation and submarine launched ballistic missiles/undersea drones.

6

STRATEGIC MISSILE FORCES DEVELOPMENT AND MODERNISATION UNDER DEFENCE PLANNING COVERING 2012-2022

In the 2010's and early 2020's, the Russian political leadership stated unequivocally that it did not consider the nation to be in a twenty first century arms race and that such should be avoided, considering a US defence budget that typically extended well into double figures times that of the Russian defence budget. Despite this, misinformation in western mainstream media appeared to be aimed at painting such a picture, with misleading statements, such as 'The announcement that Avangard [hypersonic glide vehicle] is operational heralds a new and dangerous era in the nuclear arms race. It confirms once again President Putin's focus on bolstering and modernising Russia's nuclear arsenal' (BBC News, 27 Dec 2019). This was a misleading analysis on many fronts. First Russia's modernisation of her armed forces, including the SMF (Strategic Missile Forces), was in line with the Defence Plan for 2012-2022 and not part of any nuclear arms race. Second, a nuclear arms race, in regard to strategic delivery systems, was not in progress, nor could one possibly be under the terms of the New START (New Strategic Arms Reduction Treaty) that entered into force in 2011 and remained in force in 2021 – this limited the Russian Federation and United States of America to a maximum of 1500 deployed nuclear warheads on 700 deployed launchers. When a new modern system, such as an RS-24 Yars ICBM (Intercontinental Ballistic Missile) complex, was introduced, then an older system, such as an RT-2PM Topol ICBM complex, was removed from the inventory and deactivated under the New START verification process. Third, the BBC article stated that Putin was focused on 'bolstering… Russia's nuclear arsenal' (BBC News, 27 Dec 2019), whereas the 2012-2022 plan was centred on modernising the entire Russian Armed Forces as it moved from Soviet era armaments to modern armaments, bringing it up to date with western rearmament programs that commenced in the 1990's. In this regard, it can be considered that Russia was catching up rather than pushing ahead in regard to modernising her defence potential. The advancement on capability of her strategic strike systems had been necessitated through the development and introduction of advanced missile defence systems by the United States following the termination of the ABM (Anti-Ballistic Missile) Treaty in 2002. The term bolstering could be considered proper in regard to enhancements to the Russian SMF as a nuclear deterrent in the face of NATO (North Atlantic Treaty Organisation) attempts to negate its deterrence potential through introduction of extensive ABM systems in Europe. However, in this respect, it would then have to be considered a restorative move to parity that would reduce the potential for nuclear conflict and a move away from rather than heralding the dangerous era the fallacious arms race for nuclear superiority voiced in the BBC article and repeated in 2021).

The large-scale misinformation campaign, often, perhaps with justification, referred to as xenophobia, prevalent within western mainstream media in regard to the Russian Federation unfortunately made the work of researchers working with factual information all the more difficult – a situation that was unlikely to improve in an age of mass media/social media pushing out streams of unsubstantiated/fallacious information fueling geopolitical agendas. This may have been intended to paint the Russian Federation as the World's boogeyman that had to be contained, and possibly to provide justification for western nations support for right wing ultra-nationalists whom pedal hate speech, but are fallaciously painted as liberals. This may potentially have been part of wider efforts to politically destabilise Russia, potentially through western nations threats of refusal to recognise democratic decisions of the Russian electorate through non-recognition of election results, alongside sanctions aimed at stifling economic growth, but, to a greater degree, stifling intelligent debate between those on opposite sides of geopolitics – a lose-lose situation for all parties, as political, economic and military ties are continually constrained, leaving only tension and mistrust, which, in turn, would naturally increase the scope for conflict, conventional or nuclear, through miscalculation.

Unable to influence the world political situation, the Russian SMF is tasked with preserving a retaliatory (including second strike) strategic nuclear strike capability against any adversary that attacked the country or one of her allies with nuclear weapons (for details of the conditions for Russian nuclear employment against an adversary see chapter 2). To accomplish this in the face of advanced technological threats the SMF embarked upon a large-scale modernisation program in the first decade of the twenty first century, whilst observing obligations in force under the nuclear arms control/reduction treaties (from 2011 this was New START).

Page 118: Going into the third decade of the twenty first century the SMF continued the progressive replacement of Topol and Topol-M complexes with the RS-24 Yars. Page 119: SMF PGRK regiment convoy on a patrol route in June 2020. MODRF

Under the 2012-2022 modernisation plan, the SMF would introduce new advanced missile systems (refer to previous chapters) – a new generation BZHRK (Rail mobile Intercontinental Ballistic Missile) complex was cancelled in the second half of the second decade of the twenty first century – and update other operational areas, infrastructure and organisational, such as early warning and communications and maintain and improve the high standard of operational exercises to maintain combat efficiency. A snapshot of the latter is evident through a notable increase in large-scale training operations. As an example, on 15 January 2016, five mobile ICBM regiments embarked upon a wide-ranging operation in the Tver, Kirov, Sverdlovsk and Irkutsk regions, and in the Mari El Russian Republic. During this exercise the respective regiments conducted the transit to pre-planned deployment areas for their respective Topol, Topol-M and Yars intercontinental range ballistic missile systems. Other elements of the respective regiment tasking's were conducted, such as countering sabotage and attempts to disrupt the safe movement of the missile launchers, rapid position changing and equipment concealment (MODRF, 2016). During the course of 2016, the SMF conducted in excess of 100 exercises (scheduled) – command and staff, tactic and special (MODRF, 2016a). During 2017, in excess of 100 command/staff and more than 50 tactic and special exercises were conducted (MODRF, 2017b). This had commenced with readiness deployments, involving the movement of Topol armed mobile launchers of the Bologove Missile Formation (Rezhitsa Red Banner Guards Missile Division), Tver Region, to field positions around the 11th of January 2017 (MODRF, 2017c). On the 3rd of the following month, training deployments were conducted with Topol mobile launchers of the Barnaul missile formation (MODRF, 2017d). By mid-May 2017, the SMF had conducted in excess of fifty exercises over the course of the 2016/2017 winter training period (MODRF, 2017e).

Rembat UVO3 (SEM CL) recovery vehicle delivered to a missile regiment in the Amur region of Russia. MODRF

Digital Communications – As well as the improvements to existing missile complexes and introduction of new missile complexes – Yars, Sarmat and Avangard – the SMF embarked upon modernisation of command and control systems, such as the introduction of digital communications. In 2017, the SMF introduced a new information transfer system for the positioning of mobile regiments of respective missile divisions, along with modernised satellite communications stations, modernised radio stations operating in the HF (High Frequency) and VHF (Very High Frequency) bands. The steady implementation of such systems in the respective missile divisions put the SMF on course to switch completely to digital communications before the end of 2020 – as well as the above mentioned systems, this would include digital telecommunication systems, incorporating telephone exchanges optimised for open communications and secured for classified communications, local-area networks and private data networks operated by the

MODRF. The new digital systems facilitated a notable reduction in the time required for effective decision making and overall efficiency of multi-tier communications within the SMF and their wider communications with outside organisations. Prior to introduction in the respective missile divisions, the new digital communications systems were introduced to SMF training centres and the 4th State Central Multipurpose Firing Range (Kapustin Yar) (Department of Mass Communications of the Russian Federation Ministry of Defence, 2020).

MIOM (engineering support and camouflage vehicle) developed for SMF PGRK formations. MODRF

Through the 2010's, the mobile missile divisions underwent significant enhancement of their vehicle complements. Whilst much of the equipment consisted of legacy systems carried over from previous generation mobile missile complexes, in many areas these were updated and several new systems were introduced. For example, in the region of 100 major items of equipment – automated missile launch systems, ICBM's, mobile command stations, engineering and combat vehicles, for mobile missile regiments – were supplied to the SMF in 2016 (MODRF, 2016b).

From 2015 through December 2020, the SMF had introduced in excess of thirty MIOM (engineering support and camouflage vehicles) and MDM (Leafy Foliage and Remote Mine Clearance) vehicles – these vehicles were allocated to missile divisions rearming with RS-24 Yars mobile missile complexes. The MIOM was developed to conduct engineering tasks, reconnaissance of patrol routes and field deployment sites selected for the PGRK (mobile missile) TLV (Transport Launch Vehicle). One of the major tasking's for the MIOM vehicles was assessment of the ground (soil) capacity to withstand the high load bearings of the ICBM and ensuring the dimensional (width) of route assessment and, if required, enhancement, for operation of the various vehicles in the PGRK convoy. The MDM was developed to enhance the operability and survivability of mobile missile units when traversing combat routes, and when establishing a field site, through countering remote controlled, radio controlled and stand-alone land mines (Information Group of the SMF, 2020).

In the third decade of the twenty first century, the PGRK regiments of the SMF missile divisions were equipped with a plethora of support vehicles, including the 15M107 Listva Remote Mine Disarming Vehicle tasked with clearing TLV patrol routes of threats posed by mines/improvised explosive devices that may have been planted along the route. MODRF

Infographic with basic characteristics – crewing, road range, reconnaissance, demining rate in km/h, radius of engaging mines (distance from vehicle) and mine detection depth, assuming a metal based mine – of the Listva remote controlled demining vehicle in service with the **PGRK** missile regiments/missile divisions of the Strategic Missile Forces. A single Listva vehicle, referred to as 'The Guardian Angel of Topol and Yars', could take on the tasking's previously allocated to dedicated engineering units. It would typically be positioned at the fore of the **PGRK** convoy to ensure safe passage for ICBM transporter launcher vehicle, engineering and other vehicles. Once a mine was detected by various means the devices electronics could be burnt out by a microwave-emitter rendering it useless. A decision would then be made on whether the mine should be cleared or exploded. Rostec

Top: **15M107 Listva Remote Mine Disarming Vehicle of the Strategic Missile Forces.** Bottom: The Typhoon-M anti-sabotage, chemical/biological/radioactive decontamination and reconnaissance vehicle began replacing earlier generation vehicles in Strategic Missile Forces **PGRK** regiments from 2016. MODRF

Through 2016, in the order of 70 or so items of new engineering equipment were issued to the mobile regiments of the SMF. Among these acquisitions were some twelve support and remote demining vehicles distributed among four missile formations rearming with RS-24 Yars missile complexes (MODRF, 2016c). Engineering elements of the mobile missile regiments were then scheduled to receive up to 200 new wheeled vehicles through 2020, with around 30 of these delivered during 2017. The new engineering vehicles were to replace BAT-M, BAT-2 and PKT track-layer, BKT-RK-2 bulldozers and UDM universal road vehicles (MODRF, 2017f). In 2017, the year that it completed re-equipment with RS-24 Yars, the Novosibirsk Missile formation was equipped with new generation support vehicles, including Listva remote demining vehicles, MIOM engineering support and camouflage vehicles, ARS-14KM decontamination and de-grassing vehicle (mobile spray station) and Typhoon-M. Similar re-equipment was expected within the Irkutsk and Yoshkar-Ola missile formations, which were rearmed with RS-24 Yars from 2017 through 2018 (MODRF, 2017g). Other vehicular equipment introduced to RS-24 Yars mobile units included the Rembat UVO3 recovery vehicle (MODRF).

The BPDM Typhoon-M armoured vehicles, in-excess of 70 of which had been delivered to the SMF from 2016 through summer 2021, were allocated to security, anti-sabotage, chemical/biological/radioactive decontamination and reconnaissance (radar, infrared and optical) units (Information Support Group of the SMF, 2021 & MODRF, 2020). The defence potential of the mobile SMF regiments was enhanced through addition of a new UAV (Uninhabited Air Vehicle) launch capability on the Typhoon-M and the deployment of the Peresvet combat laser system. The MODRF confirmed that the laser complexes had been placed on combat alert with five of the Strategic Missile Forces mobile missile divisions from 1 December 2019 (MODRF Speech, 2019 & Russian Defence Ministry Board Meeting, 2019).

By 2020, missile regiments of the SMF mobile missile divisions had received in the region of 100 simulators for the operation of the RS-24 Yars complex. MODRF

The updated Defence Plan for 2016-2020 was approved in November 2015. In regard to the SMF, this called for continued modernisation and maintaining 95% of deployed missile launch complexes in a state of combat alert. By late 2015, the MODRF had confirmed that six missile regiments had been armed with RS-24 Yars missile complexes, mobile and silo based, enabling the SMF to achieve a 51% value of modern missile systems in service (MODRF Board, 2015). During the course of 2016, 41 new intercontinental ballistic missiles had been delivered to the Strategic Nuclear Forces of the Russian Federation (this included RS-24 Yars for the SMF and RS-30 SLBM (Submarine Launched Ballistic Missile). The RS-24 deliveries provisioned for the SMF placement of a further four missile regiments on combat alert with Yars silo and mobile based missiles during 2016. As at 22 December 2016, around 99% of SMF missile launch systems were assessed as being combat capable, 96% of which were on combat alert (MODRF Board, 2016). By 2017, some 56% of SMF missile complexes were of modern types, three PGRK missile regiments being re-equipped with Yars during the course of that year (MODRF Results of Activities, 2017, MODRF Tasks, 2017 & MODRF, 2017h). During the course of 2018, the delivery and placement on combat alert of 11 Yars ICBM complexes facilitated for the completion of the re-equipment of the Yoshkar-Ola Missile Division. During that same year, the Korzel missile formation continued re-equipment with Yars (MODRF, MODRF Board Session, 2018 & MODRF Tasks, 2018). In mid-December 2018, it was determined that 70% of the SMF had been re-equipped with modern weapon systems under the updated 'Construction and Development Plan' for the SMF for the period 2016-2021 (Detail from Commander of the SMF, Colonel-General Sergey Karakaev, 2018). During 2019, the value for modern missile systems had reached 76% for the SMF and 82% for the Russian Strategic Nuclear Forces nuclear triad in general (SMF ICBM, naval SLBM and Long Range Aviation air launched missiles). By December 2020, the SMF missile groupings were made up of around 81% of advanced systems (SMF Communique, Dec 2020) as the MODRF pushed toward a 100% modern missile complex establishment by 2027. During 2021, the share of advanced modern weapon systems within Russian Strategic Nuclear Forces was expected to exceed 88% (State of the Nation address to the Russian Federation Federal Assembly, 2021).

In the shadow of the placement on combat alert of the first two Avangard complexes on 27 December 2019, three SMF missile regiments were re-equipped with RS-24 Yars. The defence plan for 2020 called for the delivery and activation of 22 Yars and Avangard complexes (MODRF Speech, 2019 & Russian Defence Ministry Board Meeting, 2019). The MODRF confirmed that the missile division based at Irkutsk, Siberia, had completed rearmament with Yars in September 2020 and the Russian Defence Minister, during a defence ministry conference call on 13 October that year, confirmed that two Yars complexes had been placed into missile silos at the Kaluga facility in central Russia (Defence ministry conference call, 2020). Forward planning called for introduction of thirteen Yars and Avangard complexes in 2021, and completion of infrastructure for such ICBM complexes at Kozelsk, Yasnoye, Uzhur, Novosibirsk and Yoshkar-Ola (Expanded Meeting of the Defence Ministry Board, 2020).

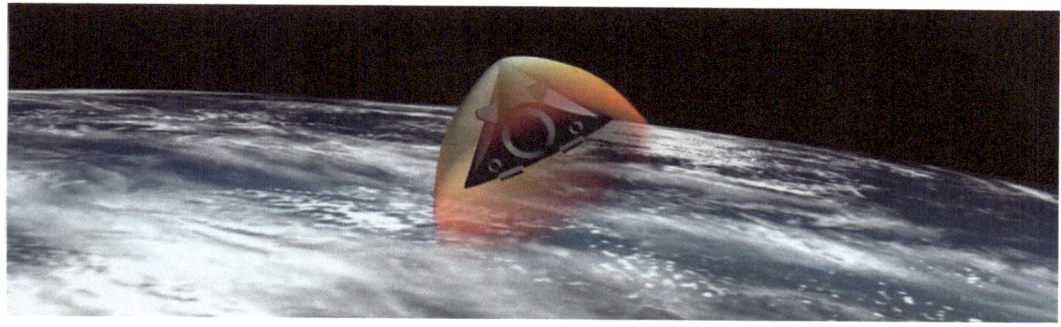

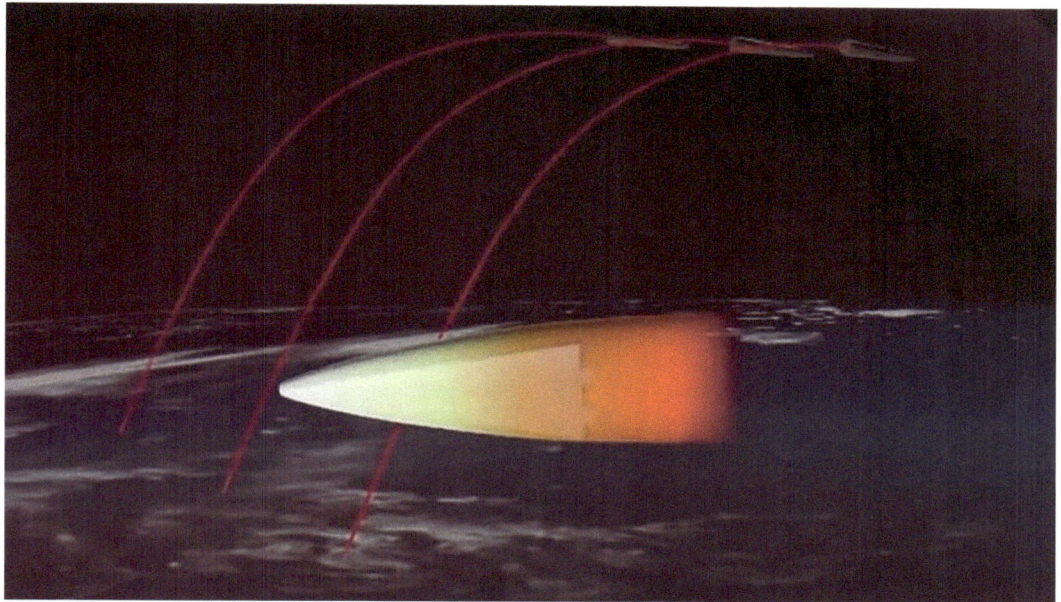

Computer generated graphics depicting Avangard hypersonic glide vehicle during the sub-orbital phase of its flight (top) and avoiding interception by ballistic missile defence interceptors (bottom). MODRF

In the period 2012-2020, the SMF conducted ten successful launches of Yars missile systems and four successful launches of ICBM's (UR-100N UTTX) carrying Avangard hypersonic glide vehicle payloads, as well as continued testing of older systems of the Topol/Topol-M family. During the same period, 2012-2020, the number of Yars missile complexes on combat alert increased tenfold whilst the number of Avangard complexes increased fourfold. In regard to Avangard, this indicated that four such systems were on combat alert by December 2020 (Main Results of the Russian Armed Forces, activities in 2012-2020, 2020).

With allocation of additional production funding, the plan for 2021 (confirmed by the Russian Defence Minister, Sergie Shoigu at the MODRF enlarged board meeting on 21 December 2020) called for the SMF to place thirteen Yars and Avangard systems on combat alert by the end of the year (noted above), by which time it was intended that some 88.3% of the SMF strategic missile complexes would consist of modern advanced systems. In addition, the necessary infrastructure modifications were to be completed at sites in Kozelsk, Yasy, Uzhur, Novosibirsk and Yoshkar-Ola, to accommodate future installation of Yars and Avangard armed missile complexes. It was expected that the first regiment (1st Missile Regiment) equipped with Avangard would attain full operational strength during late 2021 (MODRF Enlarged Board Meeting, 21 December 2020).

At the State of the Nation address to the Russian Federation Federal Assembly on 21 April 2021, it was confirmed, at presidential level, that Russia intended to place the first RS-28 Sarmat heavy ICBM complex on combat alert with a SMF missile regiment in late 2022 (State of the Nation address to the Russian Federation Federal Assembly, 2021).

RS-28 Sarmat representative test vehicle positioned atop a launch silo for test of the reactive mortar (pop-up) system that ejects the missile from the silo prior to main engine ignition. MODRF

As of December 2020, the SMF silo based missile systems consisted of R-36M2 Voevoda, UR-100N UTTKh, RT-2PM2 Topol-M, RS-24 Yars and Avangard (arming modified UR-100N UTTKh ICBM complexes. The mobile missile systems consisted of RT-2PM Topol, RT-2PM1 Topol-M and RS-24 Yars (SMF Communique, Dec 2020). Around 20 new missile complexes were typically introduced each year. These systems, in 2020, comprised Yars mobile based, Yars silo-based and Avangard, with the Sarmat heavy ICBM, as noted above, expected to be introduced in 2022 (SMF Communique, Dec 2020) as R-36M2 complexes were withdrawn – two, such complexes being scrapped in 2020 under the New START verification process.

Further modernisation entailed specific rearmament of the heavy ICBM element of the SMF with RS-28 Sarmat, continued rearmament of the light ICBM element with RS-24 (RS-26) Yars/improved Yars (Rubezh) and launch vehicles to carry Avangard hypersonic glide vehicles aloft. This would reduce the overall number of systems to be maintained on combat alert whilst ensuring and, indeed, enhancing, the retaliatory strike potential, and thus, the deterrent potential against those countenancing a nuclear strike on the Russian Federation or one of her CSTO (Collective Security Treaty Organisation) partner nations.

Looking further ahead, the commander of the SMF, in December 2020, confirmed that the Russian Federation would commence development of new strategic missile systems in the short to medium term (SMF Communique, Dec 2020) expected to be a follow on to the Yars light ICBM complex. This emerged as the Kedr strategic missile system program, unveiled in 2021 when it was in what was described as the science and development phase. This program was, in 2021, shrouded in the highest levels of secrecy, concrete information unlikely to emerge until it moves to the research & development stage, funded under the Russian Federation state armaments program up to 2027. However, it has been indicated that the solid-fueled missile would enter full-development in the 2023-2024 timeframe and could commence replacement of Yars from 2030.

An RS-28 Sarmat representative test vehicle is propelled from the entrance of an intercontinental ballistic missile test silo during reactive mortar (pop-up) ejection testing. MODRF

In late June 2021, reports indicated that a new generation ICBM (developed by the Moscow Institute of Thermal Technology), speculated in media to be Kedr, had undergone a test launch from the Plesetsk Cosmodrome, although there was no official confirmation. It is possible that this was a modification of the RS-24 Yars, apparently holding the designation RS-26, or, alternatively, it may have been a Topol series missile modified to flight test advanced technologies for integration into a next generation ICBM complex.

SMF PGRK ICBM convoy on a patrol route in June 2020 (top) and a PGRK Yars complex operating out of the Ivanovo region on 25 February 2021 (bottom). MODRF

GLOSSARY

ABM	Anti-Ballistic Missile
BBC	British Broadcasting Corporation
BZHRK	Rail Mobile Intercontinental Ballistic Missile
cm	Centimetre
CONUS	Continental United States
CSTO	Collective Security Treaty Organisation
CTBT	Comprehensive (nuclear) Test Ban Treaty
CTBTO	Comprehensive (nuclear) Test Ban Treaty Organisation
FOBS/DICBM	Fractional Orbit Bombardment System/Depressed trajectory Intercontinental Ballistic Missile
HF	High Frequency
H.Q.	Headquarters
ICBM	Intercontinental Ballistic Missile
II	Roman numeral number 2
III	Roman numeral number 3
INF	Intermediate Range nuclear Forces (treaty banning intermediate range ground launched missiles signed in 1987 and entered into force in 1988 – defunct following US suspension in February 2019, which led to the treaties demise)
IRBM	Intermediate Range Ballistic Missile
kg	Kilogram
KIK	Ground Control Station
Kiloton	1 kiloton = 1000000 kg of TNT equivalent force
km	Kilometre
km/h	Kilometers per hour
km/s	Kilometers per second
kW	Kilowatt
m	Metre
MAD	Mutually Assured Destruction
MDB	Makeyev Design Bureau
min^{-1}	Revolutions per minute
MIRV	Multiple Independently targetable Reentry Vehicle
MITT	Moscow Institute of Thermal Technology
mm	Millimetre
MODRF	Ministry of Defence of the Russian Federation
MRBM	Medium Range Ballistic Missile
MRV	Multiple Reentry Vehicle
MS	Military Space Forces
Mt	Megaton (1 Megaton = 1000000000 kg TNT equivalent force)
MW	Megawatt

NATO	North Atlantic Treaty Organisation – Alliance of major western block nations created in 1949
New START	New Strategic Arms Reduction Treaty (in effect from February 2011-February 2021 and extended, in the latter year, to February 2026)
NPR	Nuclear Posture Review
OJSC	Open Joint Stock Company
PGRK	Mobile strategic missile complex
R&D	Research & Development
SALT	Strategic Arms Limitation Treaty
SDI	Space Defence Initiative
SLBM	Submarine Launched Ballistic Missile
SMF	Strategic Missile Forces
SRBM	Short-Range Ballistic Missile
SSBN	Nuclear Powered Ballistic Missile Submarine
START	Strategic Arms Reduction Treaty – referred to as START-1 (signed between the USSR and USA on 31 July 1991 – expired on 5 December 2009)
TLV	Transporter Launch Vehicle
TNT	Trinitrotoluene – a high explosive chemical formation
UAV	Uninhabited Air Vehicle
US	United States
USA	United States of America
USSR	Union of Soviet Socialist Republics/Soviet Union
V	Volts
VHF	Very High Frequency
Warsaw Pact	Formal treaty of friendship, co-operation and mutual assistance signed between the Socialist Republics of the USSR and 7 Soviet orbit satellite states in Eastern Europe. This treaty, which took effect from 14 May 1955, was designed to counter the growing NATO alliance opposed to the eastern block
YDB	Yuzhnoye Design Bureau
%	Percent
~	Approximately equal to (can also be used to mean asymptotically equal)
°	Degree(s)

BIBLIOGRAPHY

4th State Central Interspecific Range of the Ministry of Defence of the Russian Federation (the Kapustin Yar Test Site), History, 416540, Astrakhan region, Znamensk, military unit 15644

90th Interspecific (Multi-Service) Regional (Training) Centre for the SMF (Yaroslav Region) History, 2020, MODRF Strategic Missile Forces, 52024, Yaroslavl region, Pereslavl-Zalessky, md, Chkalovsky, Military unit 74306

161st (161-I) Strategic Missile Force Technicians School (Astrakhan Region) History, 2020, Strategic Missile Forces, 416540, Astrakhan region, Znamensk, Military unit 75376

Barnaul Missile Formation (Red Banner Orders of Kutuzov and Aleksandra Nevsky Missile Division) History, 2020, MODRF Strategic Missile Forces, 658076, Altai territory, ZATO Siberian, Military unit 52929

BBC (2019) *Russia Deploys Avangard Hypersonic Missile System*, BBC News (Jonathon Marcus), 27 Dec 2019

Bologoevskoe missile compound (Guards Krasnoznamennaya Rezhitskaya Missile Division) History, 2017, MODRF Strategic Missile Forces, 171-60, Tver region, Bologoye-4, Military unit 14245

Chronology of significant dates of the Strategic Missile Forces, Ministry of Defence of the Russian Federation

Decree of the Russian Federation government defence order, and forward planning for the period covering 2012-2013

Decree passed by the Russian State Duma (Russia's Lower House of Parliament) on 21 July 2020

Detail from the department of Organisational and Technical Measures on Missile Armament, Strategic Missile Forces, Ministry of Defence of the Russian Federation, Moscow, Russia

Detail from the Organisational and Mobilisation Department of the H.Q. of the Strategic Missile Forces (WMD of the SMF)

First generation military rockets [history], Yuzhnoye Design Bureau

Fourth generation military rockets [history], Yuzhnoye Design Bureau

Harkins, H (2017) 'Orbital/Fractional Orbit Bombardment System' - *The Soviet Globalnaya Raketa*, Centurion Publishing, United Kingdom

Harkins, H (2020) 'Typhoon K', *K-63968, K-63969, K-53949 & K-4386 MRAP Armoured*

Vehicles, Centurion Publishing, United Kingdom

Information Group of the Strategic Missile Forces (2020) Release dated 27 December 2020, Information Support Group of the SMF, Ministry of Defence of the Russian Federation

Information Support Group of the SMF (2021) *Since 2016, more than 70 Typhoon-M anti-sabotage combat vehicles have been delivered to the Strategic Missile Forces*, Release dated 15 August 2021, Information Support Group of the Strategic Missile Forces, Ministry of Defence of the Russian Federation

Interspecific Regional Training Centre for the SMF [History] (Pskov Region), MODRF Strategic Missile Forces, 181353, Pskov region, Ostrov-3, military unit 35600

Irkutsk missile connection (Guards missile Vitebsk Order of Lenin Red Banner Division) History, 2017, MODRF Strategic Missile Forces, 664078, Irkutsk-35, Military unit 59968

Kozelsk (Kozelskoye) Missile Formation (Red Banner (Guards Krasnoznamennaya) Guards Missile Division) History, 2020, 249725, Kaluga region, Kozelsk-5, Military unit 54055

NPO Mashinostroyenia (2017) UR-100N UTTX Basic specification sheet, JSC Mashinostroyenia Military Industry Corporation NPO Mashinostroyenia, Reutov, Moscow region, Russia

MDB Release on Sarmat Research & Development, June 2011, JSC GRT State Rocket Centre Makeyev, named after Academican V.P. Makeev, Russian Federation

Military Academy of the Strategic Missile Force History section (accessed December 2020), Ministry of Defence of the Russian Federation

MODRF *Main Results of the Russian Armed Forces, activities in 2012-2020*, Ministry of Defence of the Russian Federation, Moscow, Russian Federation

Russian Defence Ministry Board Meeting (2019) *Defence Ministry Board Meeting at the National Defence Control Centre*, 24 December 2019, Ministry of Defence of the Russian Federation

Russian Defence Ministry Board (2015) *Key points of the report of the Russian Defence Minister at the extended session of the Russian Defence Ministry Board, 11 December 2015*, Ministry of Defence of the Russian Federation

Russian Federation (2020) *Basic Principals of State Policy of the Russian Federation on Nuclear Deterrence*, The President of the Russian Federation, Executive Order, The Ministry of Foreign Affairs of the Russian Federation, 8 June 2020

MODRF (2010) The Topol rocket struck the target at the range in Kazakhstan, Ministry of Defence of the Russian Federation release, 6 December 2010

MODRF (2015) Board Meeting, Ministry of Defence of the Russian Federation, 2015

MODRF (2016) Board Meeting, Ministry of Defence of the Russian Federation, 2016

MODRF (2016) *Five SMF missile regiments practice combat duty within with the exercise*, Release dated 15 January 2016, Ministry of Defence of the Russian Federation, Moscow, Russian Federation

MODRF (2016) *Record on the Strategic Missile Forces at October 2016*, Ministry of Defence of the Russian Federation, Moscow, Russian Federation

MODRF (2016) Release dated 1 Dec 2016, Ministry of Defence of the Russian Federation

MODRF (2016) Release dated 21 Jan 2016, Ministry of Defence of the Russian Federation

MODRF (2016) *Results of the Strategic Missile Forces in 2016*, Ministry of Defence of the Russian Federation, Moscow, Russian Federation

MODRF (2016) *SMF engineer units to receive a record number of new hardware*, Ministry of Defence of the Russian Federation release, 21 January 2016, Moscow, Russian Federation

MODRF (2016) *Statement by the Minister of Defence of the Russian Federation, General of the Army, Sergei Shoigu*, Extended Board Session of the Russian Defence Ministry, 22 December 2016

MODRF (2016) *Yoshkar-Ola formation received Yars mobile missile complexes*, MODRF 16 December 2016, Ministry of Defence of the Russian Federation, Moscow, Russian Federation

MODRF (2017) *Central Archive of the Russian Federation Ministry of Defence*, January 2017, Ministry of Defence of the Russian Federation

MODRF (2017) *Command of the Strategic Missile Forces*, Ministry of Defence of the Russian Federation, Moscow, Russian Federation

MODRF (2017) *Exercise with crews of Topol mobile ground missile complexes started in the Barnaul SMF formation*, Ministry of Defence of the Russian Federation release, 3 February 2017

MODRF (2017) Release dated 29.09.2017, Ministry of Defence of the Russian Federation

MODRF (2017) Release from Department of Mass Communications of the Russian Federation Ministry of Defence, 11.09.2017

MODRF (2017) *Results of the Activities of the Russian Ministry of Defence in 2017*, Ministry of Defence of the Russian Federation

MODRF (2017) *Rocket complex R-36M2* infographic, Ministry of the Defence of the Russian Federation

MODRF (2017) *Russian Space Forces*, Ministry of Defence of the Russian Federation release, 4 October 2017

MODRF (2017) *Short History of the Russian Space Forces*, Ministry of Defence of the Russian

Federation (accessed 4 October 2017)

MODRF (2017) *Short History of the Strategic Missile Forces*, Ministry of Defence of the Russian Federation (accessed 2017)

MODRF (2017) *SMF will receive more than 200 newest wheeled road vehicles for equipping field positions*, Ministry of Defence of the Russian Federation release, 26 January 2017

MODRF (2017) *Strategic Missile Forces*, Ministry of Defence of the Russian Federation release

MODRF (2017) *Strategic Missile Forces held more than 50 tactic and special exercises in winter training period*, Ministry of Defence of the Russian Federation release, 11 May 2017

MODRF (2017) *Structure of the Strategic Missile Forces*, Ministry of Defence of the Russian Federation

MODRF (2017) *Tasks of the Armed forces of the Russian Federation in 2017*, Ministry of Defence of the Russian Federation

MODRF (2017) Test launch of Topol intercontinental ballistic missile was held in the Astrakhan region, Ministry of Defence of the Russian Federation release, 26 September 2017

MODRF (2017) *Topol missile launchers entered the combat patrol routes in the Tver Region*, Ministry of Defence of the Russian Federation Release, 11 January 2017

MODRF (2017) *Yars missile complexes are to permanent locations after military parade in Moscow*, Ministry of Defence of the Russian Federation release, 11 May 2017

MODRF (2018) *Defence Minister of the Russian Federation addresses extended session of Defence Ministry Board Session, 18 December 2018*, Ministry of Defence of the Russian Federation

MODRF (2018) *Tasks of the Armed forces of the Russian Federation in 2018*, Ministry of Defence of the Russian Federation

MODRF (2019) Speech on Russian defence capability, Ministry of Defence of the Russian Federation

MODRF (2020) *By 2020 the SMF switch fully to digital data transmission technology*, Department of Mass Communications of the Russian Federation Ministry of Defence, 05.07.2020

MODRF (2020) *Enlarged board meeting on 21 December 2020*, Ministry of Defence of the Russian Federation, Moscow, Russian Federation

MODRF (2020) *Expanded Meeting of the Defence Ministry Board, 21 December 2020*, Ministry of Defence of the Russian Federation

MODRF (2020) *Main Results of the Russian Armed Forces, activities in the 2012-2020 period*, 2020,

Ministry of Defence of the Russian Federation

MODRF (2020) *Release from the Deputy Defence Minister of the Russian Federation*, 3 February 2020, Ministry of the Defence of the Russian Federation

MODRF (2020) *Russian Defence Minister, defence ministry conference call*, 13 October 2020, Ministry of Defence of the Russian Federation

MODRF (2020) *Russian Space Force Commander (Alexander Golovko) statement, 22 July 2020*, Ministry of the Defence of the Russian Federation

MODRF (2021) *RT-2PM Basic specification sheet*, Ministry of the Defence of the Russian Federation

MODRF (2021) *RT-2MP2/1 Basic specification sheet*, Ministry of the Defence of the Russian Federation

MODRF (2021) *R-36M2 basic specification sheet*, Ministry of the Defence of the Russian Federation

MODRF (2020) *Statement from the Russian Defence Minister, December 2020*, Ministry of Defence of the Russian Federation, Moscow, Russian Federation

MODRF (2020) *Statement from the Russian Space Force Commander (Alexander Golovko), 22 July 2020*, Ministry of Defence of the Russian Federation, Moscow, Russian Federation

MODRF 2020) Strategic Missile Forces Communique, December 2020, Ministry of Defence of the Russian Federation

MODRF (2020) *The Strategic Missile Forces continues to supply 'MIOM' and 'Leafy' for PGRK 'Yars'*, Information Group of the Strategic Missile Forces release, 27 December 2020

MODRF (2021) *UR-100N UTTX basic specification sheet*, Ministry of the Defence of the Russian Federation

MODRF Historical Archive for 3 July 1991, Ministry of Defence of the Russian Federation

MODRF Historical Archive for 11 August 1988, Ministry of Defence of the Russian Federation

MODRF Historical Archive for 25 February 1992, Ministry of Defence of the Russian Federation

MODRF Historical Archive for 30 July 1988, Ministry of Defence of the Russian Federation

MODRF Sarmat research and development contract, dated June 2011

MR-100 & MR-UR-100 UTTH (15P015 & 15P016 Missile Complexes detail specifications (accessed 2020), Yuzhnoye Design Bureau

NATO (2019) NATO and the INF, North Atlantic Treaty Organisation release dated 2 August 2019

Notifications under Provision 2, Section II, Part 4 of the New START agreement, 2021

Novosibirsk Missile Formation (Glukhov Red Banner Orders of Lenin, Suvorov, Kutuzov and B. Khmel'nitsky Guards Missile Division) History, 2020, 630095, Novosibirsk-95, Military unit 34148

Order No.720, Minister of Defence of the Russian Federation, Army General S. Shoigu, dated 14 December 2018

Omsk Missile Association (Guards Missile Berislav Khingan, twice Red Banner Order of Suvorov's Army) History, 2020, MODRF Strategic Missile Forces, 644006, Omsk, 16th Military Town

Orenburg Missile Association (Orenburg Missile Army) History, 2017, MODRF Strategic Missile Forces, 460064, Orenburg, St Mira, 3, Military Unit 29452

PDEMB, Hon. CEO, Chief Designer, Gerbert Yefremov interview, 2020

R-36 [first generation] detail specifications (accessed 2020), Yuzhnoye Design Bureau

R-36M & R-36M UTTH (15P014 & 15P018) Missile Complexes detail specifications (accessed 2020), Yuzhnoye Design Bureau

Rostec (2021) *Listva* infographic, Rostec State Corporation, Russian Federation

RS-12M (RT-2PM) Topol specification sheet, Museum of the Strategic Missile Forces, Ministry of Defence of the Russian Federation

Russian Federation (Government) (2010) *State defence order for 2010 and the planning period 2010-2013*, Decree of the Russian Federation Government

Russian Federation Presidential Decree, *No.549*, of 31 May 2006

Russian Federation Presidential Decree, *No.1239*, dated 10 December 1995

Second generation military rockets [history], Yuzhnoye Design Bureau

SMF (2018) *Detail from Commander of the SMF*, Colonel-General Sergey Karakaev, SMF, Ministry of the Defence of the Russian Federation

SMF (2020) Communique, Dec 2020, Strategic Missile Forces, Ministry of Defence of the Russian Federation

SMF (2020) Military Academy of the Strategic Missile Forces, named after Peter the Great

[History], 2020, 143900, Balashikha, Moscow region, sb, Karbysheva, 8

State of the Nation address to the Russian Federation Federal Assembly, 21 April 2021

Tagil Missile Formation (Tagil Missile Division) History, 2020, MODRF Strategic Missile Forces, 624791, Sverdlovsk region, GOST ZVATO, Svobodny, St Lenin 32, Military unit 34013

TASS (2020) Text from interview with RS-24 Yars Chief Designer at Moscow Institute of Thermal Technology, 2020

TASS (2021) News story, May 2021

Tatischev Missile Connection) (Taman Red Banner Orders of October Revolution Missile Division) History, 2020, MODRF Strategic Missile Forces, 412163, Saratov region, Tatishchevsk district, Settlement Svetly, Military unit 89553

Teikov (Teikovo) missile formation (Guards missile Order of Kuzutov Division) History, 2020, MODRF Strategic Missile Forces, 155046, Ivanovo region, Military unit 34048

Text of Speech of the Minister of Defence of the Russian Federation, General of the Army, Sergei Shoigu at Russian Defence Ministry Board Session, 24 December 2019

Third generation military rockets [history], Yuzhnoye Design Bureau

US Department of Energy (undated) The Manhattan Project, an alternative history, US Department of Energy, Office of History and Heritage Resources

USSR Council of Ministers Decree, *No.1384-615*, dated 17 December 1959

Uzhur Missile Formation (Red Banner Missile Division) History, 2020, MODRF Strategic Missile Forces, 660947, ZATO Settlement Solnechny Krasnoyarsk Territory, St Guards, 33

Vladimir Missile Association (Guards Missile Vitebsk Red Banner Army) History, MODRF, 2017, MODRF Strategic Missile Forces, 600021, Vladimir, St, Krasnoznamennaya, 47B, Military unit 43176

Volat Presentation 'MZKT-792210 chassis', Minsk Wheel Tractor Plant, Republic of Belarus

Volat Presentation 'Special Projects', Minsk Wheel Tractor Plant, Republic of Belarus

Volat Presentation 'Today and Tomorrow', Minsk Wheel Tractor Plant, Republic of Belarus

Yasnenskoe missile compound (rocket Krasnoznamennaya Division) History, 2020, MODRF Strategic Missile Forces, 462770 Orenburg region, ZATO Komarovsky, Military unit 68545

YDB (2017) Chronology of significant dates. MR-UR-100, R.36M and R-36M2 sections,

Yuzhnoye Design Bureau, Republic of Ukraine

YDB History Archive, 1976, Yuzhnoye Design Bureau, Republic of Ukraine

YDB (2017) R-36M2 Voevoda Basic specification sheet, Yuzhnoye Design Bureau, Republic of Ukraine

Yoshkar-Ola missile Formation (Compound) (Kiev-Zhitomir Orders of Kutuzov III (3rd grade) Missile Division) History, 2017, MODRF Strategic Missile Forces, 424045, Republic of Mari El, Yoshkar-Ola-45, Military unit 34096

Yurya Missile Formation (Melitopol Red Banner Missile Division), History, 2020, MODRF Strategic Missile Forces, 613648 Kirov region, Yuranskiy district, ZATO Pervomaisky (settlement

Yurya-2), Military unit 44200

Additional textual and or graphic material was supplied by the following design bureau/plants

Academican Pilyugin Centre, Russian Federation
JSC Avangard, Sofonovo, Smolensk region, Russia
JSF CDB Titan Federal Research and Production Centre 'Titan Barricades' within
JSC Corporation, Moscow Institute of Thermal Technology
Krunichev Space Production and Space Centre (part of Roscosmos State Corporation), Moscow, Russia
OSC KBKhA (Konstruktorskoe Buro Khimavtomatiky – Voronezh Rocket Engine Manufacturing Centre, Voronezh, Russian
PJSC Rocket and Space Corporation, Energia, named after S.P. Korolev
Press Service of High Precisions Systems Company
Votkinsky Zavod History Archive, Votkinsk Zavod plant, Udmurt Republic, Kirov, Russian Federation

ABOUT THE AUTHOR

Hugh Harkins FRAS, MIstP, MRAeS is a physicist/historian and author with an extensive research/study background in aeronautic, astronautic, astrophysics, geophysics, nautical and the wider scientific, technical and historical fields. He is also involved in research in the field of Scottish history, which formed an element of dual undergraduate degrees. Hugh has published in excess of sixty books, non-fiction and fiction, writing under his given name as well as utilising several pseudonyms. He has also written for several international magazines, whilst his work has been used as reference for many other projects, ranging from the aviation industry, international news corporations and film media to encyclopaedias, museum exhibits and the computer gaming industry. Hugh is an elected member of the Institute of Physics and Royal Aeronautical Society and is an elected Fellow of the Royal Astronomical Society. He currently resides in his native Scotland. Other titles by the author include:

Russian/Soviet Submarine Launched Ballistic Missiles: Nuclear Deterrence/Counter Force Strike
Russia's Strategic Missile Carrier/Bomber Roadmap 2018-2040 – PAK DA, Tu-160M2, Tu-95MSM & Tu-22M3M
Russia's Coastal Missile Shield - Bal-E & Bastion Mobile Coastal Cruise Missile Complexes
Iskander - Mobile Tactical Aero-Ballistic/Cruise Missile Complex
Orbital/Fractional Orbit Bombardment System - The Soviet Globalnaya Raketa
Counter-Space Defence Co-Orbital Satellite Fighter
Air War over Syria, Tu-160, Tu-95MS & Tu-22M3 - Cruise Missile and Bombing Strikes on Syria, November 2015-February 2016
Sukhoi T-50/PAK FA - Russia's 5th Generation 'Stealth' Fighter
Sukhoi Su-35S 'Flanker' E - Russia's 4++ Generation Super-Manoeuvrability Fighter
Sukhoi Su-30MKK/MK2/M2 - Russo Kitashiy Striker from Amur
MiG-35/D 'Fulcrum' F – Towards the Fifth Generation
Sukhoi Su-27SM(3)/SKM
Russian/Soviet Aircraft Carrier & Carrier Aviation Design & Evolution Volume 1 - Seaplane Carriers, Project 71/72, Graf Zeppelin, Project 1123 ASW Cruiser & Project 1143-1143.4 Heavy Aircraft Carrying Cruiser
Soviet Mixed Power Experimental Fighter Aircraft – Piston-Liquid Propellant Rocket Engine/Piston-Ramjet/Piston-Pulsejet & Piston-Compressor Jet Engine Designs of the 1940's
Raid on the Forth - The First German Air Raid on Great Britain in World War II
Light Battle Cruisers and the Second Battle of Heligoland Bight
X-35 - Progenitor to the F-35 Lightning II
X-32 - The Boeing Joint Strike Fighter
Boeing X-36 Tailless Agility Flight Research Aircraft
XF-103 – Mach 3 Stratospheric Interceptor Concept
North American F-108 Rapier - Mach 3 Interceptor
Convair YB-60 - Fort Worth Overcast
Into The Cauldron - The Lancaster MK.I Daylight Raid on Augsburg
Hurricane IIB Combat Log - 151 Wing RAF, North Russia 1941
RAF Meteor Jet Fighters in World War II, an Operational Log
Typhoon IA/B Combat Log - Operation Jubilee, August 1942
Defiant MK.I Combat Log - Fighter Command, May-September 1940
Blenheim MK.IF Combat Log - Fighter Command Day Fighter Sweeps/Night Interceptions, September 1939 - June 1940
Light Battle Cruisers and the Second Battle of Heligoland Bight

www.ingramcontent.com/pod-product-compliance
Lightning Source LLC
Chambersburg PA
CBHW041540220426
43663CB00003B/84